HC

Run a Successful Charity

By Nick Marr

With Claire Gillman

To my wife, Claire, and our sons,
Alex and George.

Nick Marr started charity work in 1986 with the Prince of Wales Community Venture in the North East working with young people at risk, using outdoor education for personal development. This also involved a period with The Sail Training Association working with young people on Tall Ships. He spent six years as an officer in the Parachute Regiment before returning to the charity sector as a manager, then Director of Youth Development with Fairbridge, and then Weston Spirit. In 1997, he became the Group Chief Executive of Henshaws Society for Blind People, Manchester's oldest charity. Nick lives on the edge of the West Pennines with his wife Claire, editor of this book, and has two sons at university. Nick and Claire still enjoy the challenge of the outdoors and in 2014, they will drive the length of Africa to raise funds and awareness of Henshaws' work with the visually impaired.

www.noteveryonegetstoseeafrica.org

www.henshaws.org.uk

Teach®
Yourself

Run a Successful Charity

By Nick Marr

With Claire Gillman

First published in Great Britain in 2013 by Hodder & Stoughton. An Hachette UK company.

This edition published 2013

Copyright © Nick Marr 2013

Hodder & Stoughton policy is to use papers that are natural, renewable and recyclable products and made from wood grown in sustainable forests. The logging and manufacturing processes are expected to conform to the environmental regulations of the country of origin.

Hodder & Stoughton Ltd

338 Euston Road

London NW1 3BH

www.hodder.co.uk

Acknowledgements

My thanks go to my agent, Chelsey Fox, my co-writer, Claire Gillman, and to my publisher, Sam Richardson at Hodder & Stoughton. I would also like to thank all those who contributed case studies to this book and those who shared their experiences, wisdom and expertise with me. Many people have helped me during my career in the charity sector, both fellow members of staff and volunteers, and service users. I am indebted to them.

Contents

Foreword

Simon Weston OBE

I started getting involved in charities after I got injured in the Falklands War, so it's about 31 years now. What motivated me was that so many people had given me so much in the way of kindness and support. Both small and large charities had also helped my family, for example, by making the travelling possible for them to come and visit me in hospital, because we weren't blessed with an affluent background.

I just wanted to give back to the people in my country who had given so much to me and my family. So, I'm very involved in charities now purely and simply because I realized the positive impact of things that people did for me and for my family, and it seemed selfish to keep it all to myself and not to give anything back.

From my personal perspective, I want to help to make a difference in other people's lives who, for one reason or another, are unable to make that difference themselves. They need support in some way to help them to achieve and to be able to succeed in whatever their endeavour.

I don't know how best to describe it but I get a lovely feeling from doing something without any thought of reward; the only reward is to feel good. There are so many reasons why people should get involved with a charity, and I can't think of too many why they shouldn't.

I remember when we first set up Weston Spirit, we took this one young lad and he'd never been outside of Liverpool. He was a city boy and we took him out to a farm that we were working with in the early days. He helped a lamb to be born and I've never seen a boy change so much – he went from this streetwise, aggressive, hard case to this complete gibbering kid with his eyes as wide as saucers. He'd actually physically had to get his hands on the lamb and help the lamb out because it had turned. The fact that he'd brought a life into the world changed him forever; he took a fresh view on his life and no longer wanted to be involved in drugs.

It's those simple little things that give somebody a different outlook on life. Some of the young people that I've seen charities work with, they may have thought they had it tough and bad, but when you put them into a special needs school with children with all manner of problems and issues, for example, you see them change. They realize that where they actually are in life is not as bad as others. Sometimes you need to have your eyes opened in order to help other people.

I think that to understand and enjoy winning, you have to have lost. And to understand how good life is, it helps to experience other people's sadness; and an awful lot of charities will expose you to that. It makes you appreciate where you are and it makes you appreciate what you've got and for me that was a driver to try and help.

If you're involved in charity, you know there are issues but the one thing you need to remember is that if you focus only on problems, they are all you'll ever find. You need to focus on the positivity of the impact you can have in order to break the negativity and then you'll get solutions.

Governments and large corporations are never going to change the social environment because they don't put enough effort or genuine endeavour into it. We, the people are the ones that will bring around social change, and that's why we need to encourage more people to take up the mantle of charity. However small your role, whether it's once a week or once a month, we need people involved at all levels, and it needs to be genuine commitment, and that way, together we will change things.

We need more compassion in this world and that's what charity is – it's about being compassionate, it's about caring. You've got to have a desire to make whatever changes are necessary, whatever the area, whether it's on a human, scientific, ecological, environmental or medical level.

I work with charities of all sizes and varieties, from a special needs school in Belfast, listening dogs for the deaf and a charity that helps youngsters in prisons to stop reoffending through to certain larger military and disfigurement charities and the point is I know that charity does work.

Simon Weston OBE

Introduction

Over the course of my career in the charity sector, which spans nearly 30 years on and off, I have been privileged to work with charities from the smallest to the largest and at varying stages of their development – some I have witnessed grow from their inception, others have long and illustrious histories – my current charity, Henshaws, is the oldest charity in Manchester and has just celebrated its 176th anniversary.

I have witnessed the passion, energy and excitement that those involved in charities invest in their causes and I remain astounded by people's commitment and energy. However, I would be misleading you if I did not say that there will be times when you are starting up or running your charity that it will feel no different than working for any other organization. When you are dealing with the regulations, the law, cash shortages and office politics, you might wonder why you ever got involved in the first place. But, there will be other days when a troubled young person helps another, when a blind person writes their first email or a rare piece of art is saved for posterity, and it reminds you of why you got involved.

And the charity sector is special. The way charities bring people together and give voice to those who need it most, and the power charities have to connect people with the opportunity to make a positive difference with their time or money – these things are special and make being involved with charities a distinctive experience. While private companies have the primary purpose of making a profit and statutory bodies are dealing with the daily provision of services, charities have the opportunity to think differently. We have to keep asking ourselves how effectively do we deliver on our mission and make a distinctive impact – charities have the specialist knowledge, commitment and enthusiasm to tackle problems within the community, society, and our environment.

Another unique advantage of the charity sector is our independence. Backed by our supporters and donors, we are in a position to express an opinion, to have a voice to help the powers-that-be to understand a need, to ask the essential questions and to represent the rights and wishes of the cause or those groups that we champion. Although charities are increasingly adopting the best practices of the commercial sector in the ways they run their business, they remain proudly independent.

How to use this book

Of course, to be able to do this essential work and to be of the best service, you must first be able to make sure your charity is successful. And this is where this book comes in. I have focused on the key issues that affect you as you start up and run your charity, irrespective of its size. The intention is that the advice is straightforward and grounded in my own practical experience from hands-on charity worker to chief executive. It simplifies some of the incomprehensible jargon that proliferates in the charity world, and tries to make each aspect of running a charity easy to understand and to implement.

Undoubtedly, running a charity is challenging, especially in the current economic climate. Plus the stakes are higher if you do not succeed, because it will leave a large hole in the lives of those you help or the cause you support. Nonetheless, it is worth rising to the challenge.

And you will not be alone. You will be surrounded by enthusiastic, dedicated and passionate people. Not only those who work alongside you but the countless volunteers who give of their time and expertise so generously and tirelessly. Volunteers are the real heroes of the voluntary sector and they come from every sort of social and economic background – from celebrities and royalty to ex-cons and reformed characters. There are 23 million volunteers in the UK and they are part of the essential fabric that binds together the 162,000 charities currently operating – people getting involved because they want to make a difference and to put something back. Trustees are volunteers and you will see that charities cannot run without them.

I have met some fantastic people over the years of working with charities – people who have donated their time and challenged themselves to give to others. They are supportive of others who want to do similar work – so you will be able to benefit from the knowledge and experience of those who have gone before in the sector. Don't just take my word for it – look at all those who have contributed to the development of this book by supplying case studies in every chapter.

Doubtless, there will be times when reading this book when you wonder whether it will be worthwhile – the paperwork, the legal requirements, the liabilities and responsibilities. It may well weigh heavily on you on occasions and it will almost certainly be a challenge, but I know I speak for the majority of charity workers when I say believe us all – it will be worthwhile.

The Teach Yourself Breakthrough series has a number of features to help you get the most out of reading this book.

Run a Successful Charity includes the following boxed features:

 Remember this boxes give extra advice and information.

 Try it now boxes to provide you with useful exercises and strategies.

 Case studies to provide more in-depth introduction to a particular example.

 Focus points at the end of each chapter to help you hone in on the core message of each chapter.

 Next steps section summarizes the chapter and links to the new one.

At the end of the book you will also find a list of resources providing further information and help.

Case study: Stewart McCombe, volunteer fundraiser for Royal Manchester Children's Hospital Charity and Henshaws Society for Blind People

When my eldest son, Duncan, was 12 years old, he was diagnosed with a brain tumour. To use a cliché, this changed my life forever – for the better.

I had an incredible opportunity during Duncan's illness to experience an entirely new environment. I was suddenly communicating with world-class medical teams, including oncologists and neurologists. This communication was under the most incredible stress possible, i.e. the potential of losing one of your children. Every conversation was underpinned by trust, with a shared commitment with the NHS professionals to ensure everyone was focused on Duncan's full recovery.

During this time, I noticed, however, that some children lacked family support, young lives being entrusted to medical teams without a strong family network to provide emotional support. I was concerned to discover that not all children in Manchester could rely on family at such a key time in their lives. I realized that I wanted to do what I could to invest in the young people of Manchester.

After Duncan's time in hospital, the motivation to fund raise for charity was obvious, and raises the common theme of personal connection. To give time, and ask others to give money, the charity needs a strong emotional bond, often created through a personal experience, either direct or indirect.

My fundraising started by supporting Royal Manchester Children's Hospital (RMCH) Charity. This was not immediately after Duncan's illness. It took a long time to decide how we would give back, and although Duncan had been/is supported by both the children's hospital and The Christie, we decided to focus on one charity.

It is important to have people around you, immediate family and colleagues, who understand your purpose and at the very least give you the motivation to carry on. In my own experience, Duncan was fundamental, along with my wife, Ali, and our other children. Of equal importance, my colleagues, who had supported me during Duncan's illness, were now ready to get behind me in my efforts. Eighteen months after Duncan's recovery, we all worked as a team across the Great

Manchester Run series, to raise £12,500 for RMCH Charity. This has left a permanent legacy on the wall at the hospital entrance, which allows me a smile each time I walk into the building.

At the end of 2009, the opportunity arose to leave my banking career and explore other interests, a major part of which was getting involved in the charitable sector. The key decision I made at this time was to allocate the amount of voluntary time I would give. I allocated 20 per cent of the working week. This meant I could make clear decisions around becoming involved with charities, as working voluntarily can grow very quickly. Maintaining a limit gave me a very clear decision-making process. I had decided to identify some charities where I would like to become a trustee. I felt my banking/ commercial skills could add greater value to charities than fundraising. At this time, I was introduced to Henshaws Society for Blind People.

I was introduced to the Henshaws senior management, and quickly began to understand the passion and commitment that was creating incredible outputs from Manchester's oldest charity. Although I had not experienced any form of sight loss, I was introduced to the organization through one of its Trustees, who herself had lost her sight in adult life. By putting myself in her position, in a business role in a city centre, I quickly engaged with the team and wanted to learn more.

The roots of Henshaws, being created by a local business leader in the 1800s, made it all the more captivating. I met with the chief executive officer (CEO), chair and other trustees. I observed at a couple of board meetings, and the discussion quickly moved to being invited to consider a position on the board, playing to my strengths. I was reluctant because of my other charity commitments but passion influenced my decision. Rather than decline the invitation, we looked at another way. The CEO knew that I had limited time available, and that a routine board position would absorb this time, and more. We therefore agreed to free me from this responsibility, and focus purely on corporate engagement, taking the Henshaws story to businesses, forging links with business people, which is perhaps my core strength. This has undoubtedly been a win/win situation, born from clear goals shaped by passion and time.

Meanwhile, under the banner of the Many Hands Campaign for RMCH Charity, I committed to give business consulting to small businesses. The offer was simple. I give a day's consulting to a business; they provide the venue/resources and commit their time, and they also donate a minimum of £100 to RMCH Charity (a significant discount to my daily costs).

I do believe that fundraising and charitable involvement can sit comfortably alongside business. The fundraiser has to recognize that their passion may not be reflected in others, but for me, working with local Manchester businesses, and being able to share a personal success story with Duncan, offered a comfortable fundraising idea.

Finally, when asking people to donate personally, I set the challenge with the family that we had to 'up our game' each time we made 'the ask'. In 2012, this culminated in Duncan, my wife and myself all taking part in the Great Manchester Run, Cycle and Swim, setting challenges for each of us that were new and beyond anything we had achieved before. This was a great success, both personally and for fundraising, allowing us to generate a further £1,000 for RMCH Charity. Moreover, we are creating a wealth of memories which also make us stronger as a family.

Although I continue my charitable work, I have now returned to financial services, and I bring a much broader experience to my new role from my exposure to a range of charities. This can only be good news for everyone.

The opportunities to get involved with charities are varied, whether fundraising or using your own skills to enhance the organization. Since 2009, fundraising and being involved with charities has become a core part of my life. I have received so much back in return, in terms of learning, fulfilment, networking, fun and above all, friendship. I firmly believe that I am in credit from my charitable activities, despite the time I have consciously chosen to invest. My relationships have been, and still are, a two-way street, and I am fortunate to be enjoying my own personal development along the way.

1

First things first

In this chapter, you will learn:

▶ *Whether you need to start a charity*
▶ *Is this work already being done elsewhere?*
▶ *Are you cut out to run an organization?*
▶ *Is the time right to start up?*
▶ *How can you best help your service users?*

The great thing about people who set up and run charities is the energy and the passion that they bring to the venture. If you are reading this book, you are almost certainly committed to helping a specific sector of the community or you are passionate about a particular cause or an issue, and you want to make a difference.

Undoubtedly, you will have your own very personal reasons for wanting to set up and run a charity. And while I do not question your intentions, nonetheless there are certain frank questions that you should ask yourself before getting started, if you are to do the best work for the subject that is so close to your heart.

Do you need to set up a charity?

Whatever the subject that you espouse, setting up a charity is not always necessarily the best way to serve that cause – and occasionally it is not even legally possible.

A charity has a legal status as a specific form of voluntary organization. The first thing that distinguishes a charity is that it must benefit the public as opposed to a specific individual – and the aims, purposes and objectives of your charity must conform to the legal definition of charitable (see Chapter 3). There are other criteria that have to be met (also dealt with in detail in Chapter 3), none of which are too difficult to understand or insurmountable but sometimes, such requirements may limit what you hope to achieve, and there may possibly be a better alternative for you and your venture.

BELOW THE RADAR ENTERPRISES

Once your charitable venture has an income of £5,000 or more, you are required by law to register with the Charity Commission. However, there are plenty of groups and small organizations that do not have that level of funding, but that still fulfil an important role at community level, for example.

These smaller grassroots groups and 'volunteer led' social organizations such as faith groups, arts groups, minority or ethnic focus groups, rural groups and community groups are known within the third sector as 'Below The Radar' or BTR groups, and they have an important role to play. Most importantly, in the context of this chapter, might your venture be better suited to having a BTR-style set-up?

A recent report by the Third Sector Research Centre (TSRC) concluded that BTR groups are '... driven by need, responding to gaps in mainstream provision, sharing common interests, acting holistically and flexibly, using resources sourced internally, a key factor is that they base their actions upon their own distinctive local, and specific, knowledge that can only result from lived experience. They also operate using social networks only available to those who share experience or geography.'

One of the biggest advantages of operating as a BTR is that your venture is largely free of the burden of bureaucracy and targets that can sometimes prevent flexible and holistic responses by larger charities. You can respond to specific needs as they arise – needs that may be unmet because of lack of resources, or the failure of the state and other agencies to identify them.

You may well still feel that your cause has a broader remit, perhaps a national or international appeal, that would be best served by becoming a registered charity, but before we look at some of the qualities required by those who set up a charity, let's briefly consider some other situations where going down the route of setting up a new charity may not be the best way forward, even if it were possible.

OTHER OPTIONS

If you want to set up a charity to help an individual who is suffering from a rare disease or disorder, you would have to broaden your remit. In order to qualify for charity status, you would have to consider how the money you raise and the services you offer might also benefit others in similar circumstances, rather than just the one individual.

In the case of wanting to help an individual, you could look at setting up a non-charitable trust fund to benefit that specific person(s) or perhaps you might prefer to sink your energies into and feel funds could be donated more efficiently by supporting an existing charity that is already researching into or benefiting sufferers of their condition, for example.

When a national or international disaster occurs, it is only natural to want to help and, for various reasons or due to personal connections, sometimes people feel drawn to setting up a new charitable appeal fund rather than contributing donations or volunteering for an existing charity.

This is an option but it takes time and if you want to respond quickly to a disaster, it may be better to find an appeal that suits your ideas, and to offer money or services to that charity. For example, the Disasters Emergency Committee is an umbrella organization which launches and co-ordinates responses to major disasters overseas. It enables the British public to donate to British aid agencies who provide effective and swift humanitarian assistance in the disaster area wherever it may be in the world.

It is a very natural instinct to wish to commemorate someone by setting up a charity in their name. However, if there is an existing charity operating in that area of expertise, it may well be a better idea to create a separate, named fund within that existing charity. In that way, you still honour your loved one, their name is commemorated but you do not waste any energy or funds on duplicating what is already in existence.

You can check out if there is a charity already established for a particular condition, disease or situation by using the Register of Charities from the Charity Commission for England and Wales, or the Office of the Scottish Charity Regulator.

Sometimes the motivation for setting up a charity comes when your life has been touched or transformed by a particular issue and you want to help others who find themselves in a similar situation. A new charity might be appropriate but, yet again, collaborating with an existing charity may be a better option.

Another interesting option could be to use the services of a charity such the Charities Aid Foundation (CAF). They can set up a Managed Trust Account for you, and as a subsidiary fund of an established charity the same charitable tax benefits will apply. You can then fundraise and place proceeds in the Managed Trust Account, and you tell CAF which charitable purposes you would like the money to go towards.

You cannot set up a charity with a political purpose. That's not to say that a charity cannot undertake campaigning or political activities in order to achieve one of its charitable purposes, but it is not possible to have political aims. If you want to make a difference in society by pursuing a political aim, whether it is to oppose a new runway at an airport or to change legislation on gay marriage, you would be better served setting up a pressure group or a non-charitable campaigning body. If you applied to become a charity with such a political aim, your application would be rejected.

If you have considered all of the above, and you still feel sure that you would like to set up and run a charity, then there are just a few more considerations that I would urge you to take into account before you commit.

Remember this: Lottery funding

You do not have to be a registered charity to be accepted for a lottery grant. If you want to apply for lottery funding, check out the various different lottery grants' distributors to see what their grant eligibility requirements are (see Useful Addresses at the end of this book), but most will consider Below the Radar grassroots organizations, voluntary and community groups, without the need for charitable status. Be aware that lottery funding takes time and a lot of effort and is often not successful.

Try it now

Irrespective of whether you have finally decided that setting up a charity is the right thing to do, why not investigate how many existing charities are already operating in your area of interest, using the Charity Commission's register. You will probably be pleasantly surprised to know what services already exist and who is competing for funds.

Are there existing charities serving the same purpose?

According to the Charity Commission, there are around 180,000 registered charities, and the latest National Council of Voluntary Organizations Almanac Data suggests there are just as many smaller voluntary organizations (VOs). In all probability, there will be one or more of these organizations doing the kind of charitable work that you may have in mind for your new charity.

In the current economic climate, that means that there are a lot of charities and VOs all competing for limited funding, which is in shorter supply at this time – CAF research shows certain areas of funding are down 20 per cent from 2012 to 2013. Added to which, the public, local authorities and other funding organizations tend to prefer to give to charities with an established track record or a recognized name.

All of this will make it harder for a new charity to establish itself. And some would argue that charitable donations could be put to better use if charities pooled their resources and expertise, and if they worked more closely together.

If you have found through your research that there are existing charities in your chosen area, how would you feel about joining forces with them? In my experience, there are distinct advantages when charities in the same field collaborate (see Chapter 12).

Perhaps your energies would be better utilized if you became a trustee or volunteer for an existing charity, especially if there is a large area of overlap and duplication between the existing charity and what you are planning to do with your own venture.

Maybe your charity idea is sufficiently original or different from existing charities that you feel you would still like to pursue the idea of setting up your own charity. Even if that is the case, don't rule out the idea of working alongside existing charities so that you can make the most effective use of all your resources and give the best possible service to your combined beneficiaries. Help for Heroes is a recent success and it does not deliver services itself but raises money and gives it to those who do.

Remember this: Invaluable experience

If you spend several years devoting your skills and energies to an existing charity, not only will you gain invaluable insight and experience, but you may then feel that there is room for another charity with a slightly different emphasis or indeed a specialism that is not being covered. Perhaps then is the time to start your charity, by which time, you will have learnt the ropes and cut your teeth under the guidance of another charity.

Are you cut out to run an organization?

Let's face it; we're not all natural-born social entrepreneurs and not everyone who feels passionate about wanting to make a difference or wanting to start a worthy cause is cut out for running a charity. In my experience, the type of people who start and run charities have great enthusiasm, charisma and energy and they often have an encyclopaedic knowledge of the specialist area of their chosen cause. All of this passion is valuable and necessary when setting up but once established, it can rapidly lead to problems if, despite all their efforts, they hate figures, keep the accounts on post-it notes and receipts in various envelopes around the house and are technophobic. The days of being able to run a charity out of a biscuit tin are long gone.

It is by no means essential that you come from an accounting or business background – those skills can be bought or bartered into the organization or acquired over time and sometimes professionals offer pro bono work to charities – but you do at least need to recognize that there are areas of critical support that need to be addressed and, with the best will in the world, you and a couple of valiant mates/supporters are not going to be able or qualified to do it all alone.

Your strength as the founder almost certainly lies in the core work, garnering support and in service delivery. Yet, in order for your charity to function effectively, there are other areas that will need some serious attention and input and these may be roles that you find difficult or do not enjoy. The following are some of the key support functions that you will have to cover or get others to undertake:

STRATEGY

Have you thought beyond the initial desire to help others by setting up a charity? That was not meant to sound patronizing but having a strategic plan for outlining the goals you wish to achieve is a subject close to my heart – it is a case of looking at the bigger picture rather than focusing on the day-to-day running of the charity. If you are constantly fire-fighting and reacting to outside impetus because you and your friends/colleagues are simply spread too thin, then who will take on the responsibility of holding and chasing the vision of what you want your charity to achieve?

FINANCIAL MANAGEMENT

I don't just mean keeping an eye on the petty cash and paying the bills promptly. There has to be a greater transparency in the way that a charity handles its accounts because ultimately the public and grant bodies want to know how the money they have entrusted to you is being spent. Your 'books' or accounts will have to show that you conform to 'best practice' and they should be fit for inspection or audit at all times, and, if appropriate, posted on the Charity Commission website.

GOVERNANCE

You can only be a one-man band where everyone turns to you for a decision on everything from buying coffee to appointing staff for so long before chaos ensues. As the driving force behind the charity, you will have a vision about its purpose. Realistically, you also need others to help the organization to achieve that 'charitable purpose'. Effectively, this is what the 'governance' of a charity amounts to – it is the legal and financial responsibility of you and your board of trustees to make sure that the charity is responsibly run in order that it may best perform the work you originally set out to do, and that the charity's assets are spent responsibly and efficiently. By law, the trustees – sometimes known as directors – are accountable if this is not the case. So this is not a role to be undertaken lightly.

TECHNOLOGY EXPERTS

Information technology is a reality of running a modern charity. Love it or hate it, it's a fact of life that you will need someone with some technical know-how who can step into the breach when there is the inevitable problem with a computer, the internet, wireless connections or the myriad of other technical issues that can arise. It's not the best use of your time to be tinkering with a troublesome laptop, even if you have the inclination or expertise, but someone has to be able to do so.

FUNDRAISING AND MARKETING

These are the areas that most people associate with setting up and running a new charity but, by and large, sponsored events, tin rattling and other cash-generating ideas are something volunteers can help with. Your efforts and those of your staff may be better directed towards nurturing a relationship with those who donate and keeping them interested and involved so that they feel a link with your charity and what it achieves. This is a heady mix of marketing, publicity, fundraising and donor relations that will produce long-term results.

Remember this: Expert help

Although you may not have all the credentials needed to successfully run a charity, there is a whole host of business professionals out there who are only too happy to offer their assistance and know-how to a fledgling charity for a cause that they care deeply about. Make use of such a support network and never be frightened to ask – if you don't ask, you don't get.

Good timing?

There are probably those who would say that there is never a right time to launch a new charity, but it is perhaps worth making the point that the current social, economic and political climate has got many small, and for that matter large, charities with their backs against the wall. During hard times, charity giving naturally falls and public funding is in shorter supply, so consider very carefully whether now is the best time to be launching your venture.

If you decide to go ahead, then perhaps you should think more creatively about ways people can contribute. Should you be looking at ways to encourage in-kind contributions rather than cash donations from those who are feeling the pinch?

Personal cost

Setting up a charity requires a huge time commitment from the founding members. Once your organization is established, you will have paid staff who will work standard hours (and often beyond) but until then, everything depends on volunteers who give of their time generously but who also have other commitments on their time.

Realistically, a lot of the responsibility and work will fall to you and, even if you are diligent about apportioning your time and having a break, the new charity will be constantly on your mind. I have seen many organizers of new charities who try to do too much and, in the process, become exhausted. Sadly, they often become less and less effective too.

This does not have to be the case. Through prudent delegation of tasks and responsibility, you can prevent burnout which not only damages you but can also injure the new organization. Nonetheless, you should go into this with your eyes open – initially at least there will not be many people with enough experience/expertise to whom you can delegate, so the onus will fall on you, and your time commitment as a founder will be considerable. This can only continue for so long – as the organization grows and more people come on board, so you can take a step back to recharge your batteries, and to be in a position to take more of a strategic approach to developing the charity.

Try it now

Take a few minutes to tally up the number of calls on your spare time that you simply cannot neglect and then see how much time is left for the new venture. Can you schedule in specific time slots for charity activity? If not, you may find the demands of running such a venture will encroach on other areas of your life.

Something must be done

If, having considered all the options and the commitments involved, you still have your heart set on setting up a new charity, then this book can offer advice to help you to achieve your goals. Whatever your charity ambitions might be, you are about to get involved with something extremely worthwhile that will be challenging and rewarding in equal measure.

Case study: Daniel Dowen, Orthopaedic Surgeon, on the set-up of Pete's Pancreatic Project:

My father was diagnosed with a mass in his pancreas in September 2011, shortly after he had retired. As a medical professional, this immediately sparked a degree of fear in me as to what this could be. It was thoroughly investigated and he had a biopsy taken which came back showing that this was a malignant cancer. He underwent immediate surgery. The histology that came back from the tissue sample showed that this was a bizarre and very rare type of pancreatic cancer, called Acinar cell cancer (ACC), which makes up less than 1 per cent of cancers.

That was in December, and I got married in January, so it was a very emotional time. We looked at everything in the medical literature about this type of tumour and what the prognosis and treatment was, and there was so little out there that I felt a little unhappy about the fact that they were going to give my father a lot of chemotherapy, because there was no evidence base for doing so.

He was given all this chemo and he was so unwell that they had to stop. The decision was made that, because he'd been so unwell and because there was no evidence to support what they were doing, the chemotherapy would be withdrawn.

We decided at that point to do something specifically to research Acinar cell tumours. I started asking around and speaking to other people about the potential to set up a charity ourselves to try to fund some research into the disease. So I spoke to a friend of mine who works in the Freeman Hospital who does a lot of charity work. She also had cancer herself, so she became heavily involved in our cause because of the personal aspect, but also because she understood the business aspect. She offered to get involved in setting up a panel of people who would then set up the charity.

However, after I sought advice from you (Nick Marr), which was extremely helpful, I looked at the relevant websites recommended for charity advice. I did a lot of background reading and research and, in consultation with my parents, we decided that setting up a charity would be difficult for us. It's like setting up a small business – you need bank accounts and people to run it; it's not something you can set up and then sit back, it requires constant attention. I didn't feel I had the time to do all this and the rest of the family were busy too. Also, we wanted to spend time with Dad.

I spoke to his surgeon, as I had worked in that department and I knew him. He suggested that it might be more beneficial to do something under the Newcastle-upon-Tyne registered charity, which already has a registered number and is basically already set up. He suggested that many other people had come to similar conclusions, and they had set up specific small trust funds under the umbrella of the named charity. You have to specify this or else the money raised can go into a big pot and it might end up being spent on hospital beds, etc. So you have to specify in the trust fund what it is to be spent on – in our case, research into Acinar cell tumours.

We had to decide on a name for the trust. So we set up Pete's Pancreatic Project under the umbrella term of the Dowen Trust Fund, and we set up a website and a Just Giving page. After that, we started publicizing it and organizing a load of charity fundraising ideas and events. We put them on the website and that's how it all started.

The target that we want to raise is £100,000 because, having dabbled in medical research myself, I know that you need to pay someone a salary and for materials in order to get results. I wrote letters and sent them off to local businesses and companies. We have raised about £55,000 so far. Someone took it upon themselves to ring around every hospital in the UK that sees patients with this, and they reckon there are only 20–30 or so specimens in the whole of the UK, including my father's. We hope to get them all together under one roof and then to subject them to different chemotherapy and work out how they respond. This would have the added benefit of helping others who present with this diagnosis but also, if Dad relapses, they will know which chemotherapies he will respond to. Unfortunately, this cancer could come back at any second.

This is not something that you would ever get funding for normally because the numbers are too small. No one is interested in spending money on this research because it is not financially viable compared to breast, colon and other really common cancers.

The first series of experiments should be starting in the next few months at the Freeman Hospital in Newcastle, once it's been through the research and ethics department. And that feels really worthwhile.

Focus points

First ask yourself, is a new charity required or can I contribute meaningfully to an established organization?

If you set up a charity, there are restrictions on who and how you can help.

Not everyone is suited to running a charity – are you the right sort of person and do you have the time to devote?

You must have some skilled people around you who are willing to be involved at the outset to cover key tasks.

Next step

Having established that setting up a charity is the right way forward, whether you register it or not, in the next chapter, we'll look at some of the various options open to you.

2

Getting started

In this chapter, you will learn:

- ▶ *What the various types of charity organizations are*
- ▶ *How to decide on your charity purposes*
- ▶ *Where to get help and advice*
- ▶ *How to complete your constitution*
- ▶ *How to choose a charity name*
- ▶ *What type of governing document your charity will need*

So you have looked at the possibility of fundraising for, donating to or volunteering for one of the existing charities, and dismissed that as not being the best use of your skills or fitting your brief, but what sort of organization should you think about setting up if you are still keen to start a charity?

First and foremost, you need to establish if your proposed organization can be classified as a charity. Regardless of whether your charity will be registered with the Charity Commission or not, legally, it has to be set up wholly and exclusively to carry out charitable purposes in order to qualify. It also needs to exist for the public benefit (see Chapter 4).

There is a whole list of charitable purposes published by the Charity Commission, including the relief of poverty, needs relating to youth, age, ill-health, disability and financial hardship, as well as the advancement of education, religion, health, citizenship/community, the arts and culture, amateur sport, animal welfare, and environmental protection. The complete list can be found on the Charity Commission's website.

The easiest option is to study the list of existing categories that are already recognized by law as charitable, and then make sure that your planned activities fit the bill. If you are not sure or if your chosen field is borderline, then you may be best seeking legal advice – see Useful addresses at the end of the book for legal firms/websites set up to help fledgling charities.

If you want to pursue activities whereby only some of them are charitable, then you would not be able to set up a charity but you could probably set up a non-charitable entity – the trendy term is a social enterprise. This could be formed as a not-for-profit organization for the benefit of the community, for example, a community interest company (CIC – see below), or it could be a wholly commercial company. Either way, you can still donate some or all of the profits to charity.

Types of charity

Now you need to decide what kind of charitable organization your venture needs to be. Basically, there are three main types:

CHARITABLE TRUST

Setting up a charitable trust is the most straightforward option. Most small charities that don't have any significant trading activity and don't have members choose this option. It is not a corporate body but it is an excellent way of making sure money goes to a particular charitable purpose.

UNINCORPORATED CHARITABLE ASSOCIATION

This is the most common form of charitable organization within the voluntary sector. It is cheap to set up and can be run with relative informality and flexibility. Unlike companies, unincorporated associations are not generally subject to outside legal control. That means that there is no central register of unincorporated associations and no central regulator. Nor is there any requirement for how such an association is run or reporting obligations.

Having said that, there are key criteria established by case law, namely that an association should:

▶ Consist of two or more people with a common non-business purpose

▶ Have contractual relations between those persons

▶ Be governed by rules

▶ Be non-temporary.

Although it is not legally required, most associations have written rules to clarify the purposes of the association, to protect the management, and so that disputes between members can be avoided. This model is attractive if you don't intend to trade, for example, a local community group.

CORPORATE CHARITIES

For those charities that want to act more like a business, to fundraise, borrow money, perhaps own property or open a number of charity shops, to employ staff and enter into contracts, etc., it is sensible to set up a corporate body. In this way, you can offer a degree of protection to the trustees and staff of the charity, as this type of set-up limits their liability somewhat.

Corporate charities can be established in several ways, the most common of which are as follows:

▶ Charitable company limited by guarantee (CLG)

This is a private company, very similar to a private company limited by shares, but it cannot generate any income through the sales of its membership interests. This type of corporate structure is often chosen by charitable and non-profit organizations such as clubs, community enterprises and some co-operatives.

The downside of this model is that a CLG falls within the requirements of both company law and charity law. As such it is required to register its constitutional documents and any additional filings with both the Charity Commission and the Registrar of Companies.

▶ Charitable incorporated organization (CIO)

A charitable incorporated organization is a new legal form for a charity that was only passed by Parliament at the tail end of 2012. CIOs have all the advantages of a corporate structure, for example reduced risk of personal liability, without the need for dual regulation, as CIOs only have to register with and report to the Charity Commission.

CIOs are incorporated and operate as separate legal entities. The reporting, filing and accounting requirements for CIOs should be less of a burden than for other companies and costs are also reduced because CIOs don't have to file documents with Companies House (which charges), rather filing them solely with the Charity Commission which does not charge.

You can choose from two distinct types of CIOs: the 'foundation' model, where the charity trustees are the only members of the CIO, and the 'association' model, where there is a body of members who are distinct from the charity.

As this is a relatively new form of charity, it is expected that many existing charitable companies, unincorporated associations and charitable industrial and provident societies will want to convert to a CIO, and so there is detailed guidance available from the Charity Commission website on this procedure.

Try it now

If you are interested in setting up a CIO, you can download model forms of constitution from the Charity Commission website, which makes the whole process considerably easier.

▶ Community interest company (CIC)

Although this is not strictly a charitable company, it is an option perhaps worth considering under this heading. A CIC is in fact a limited liability company, which can be limited either by shares or guarantee. In addition, it must have the specific purpose of providing a benefit to a community. If you set up a CIC, its income, assets and profits must be used for the benefit of the community it was set up to serve, rather than for the benefit of the company's shareholders, directors and employees. A CIC is a good mix of social purpose and commercial activity and is an ideal model for schemes such as environmental improvement projects, community transport operations and fair trade.

In order to become a CIC, a company must pass the 'Community Interest Test', which means it must be able to demonstrate that a reasonable person would consider its activities to be for the benefit of the community or a section of the community.

It is important to note that a CIC is NOT a charitable company, even if its objects are entirely charitable in nature. A charitable company can become a CIC with the Charity Commission's consent, but it then loses its charitable status. Unlike the other corporate charity options we've discussed, a CIC does not have trustees; it has directors who can receive a reasonable remuneration. There is no limit on the level of profit a CIC can make because all profit is used for the benefit of the community it was set up to serve. For more information on this model, go to the Community Interest Companies website at www.cicregulator.gov.uk

Remember this: Ongoing responsibilities

Once you have become a charity, there's no going back. Even if your charity is wound up, for whatever reason, any surpluses must be given to another charity. You will have to ensure that the organization always complies with its charitable objects, and achieves public benefit. These are serious long-term responsibilities for trustees and staff and not to be undertaken lightly.

Remember this: Changing status

If you are an existing charitable trust, unincorporated association or charitable company, you can still apply to the Charity Commission in order to convert to become a CIO, provided yours is not an exempt charity.

Remember this: Budgeting

There are always start-up costs involved in setting up a new charity but when doing your projections, don't forget to factor in the fees for taking legal and tax advice about charitable status, and getting assistance in registering your charity, if you think this might be required.

Setting up your charity

Now you have given some thought to the type of charity organization you would like to be, let's look at how you go about setting up your charity.

KEEPING IT SMALL

For those of you who have decided to keep your operation small, with an income of less than £5,000 per annum, you will want to set up your charity with a constitution, although this option is not recommended for small charities that own a building or employ staff.

The Charity Commission and many national charities produce a model constitution that you can adopt. Charities that include student unions, parent teacher associations, playgroup networks, women's institutes, community football clubs, village halls (ACRE), church groups, and scouts and guides all appear on the Charity Commission's list of Approved Governing Documents. This is available on their website, and you should contact them directly for advice and model forms if you are setting up a charity in one of these areas. It's actually easier than most people think.

▶ The constitution

When setting up your small charity, the constitution (also known as the governing document) outlines the rules by which the charity is run. It also states what the charity is set up to do (its objects), how it is structured and how it might change with time. Your constitution is a legal document and it is important to get it right – people donating to the charity want their money to be spent on their cause.

Once everybody involved in setting up the charity has discussed what the charity has been set up for – the Purposes – and the rules, then these can be written into the constitution. You might also want to include the spread (local, national, international) in which the charity will operate.

Having a constitution alone is not enough to necessarily guarantee you charity status. To be a charity, all your purposes must be charitable (see next chapter) and the organization must be established for the public benefit.

Once you are happy with the constitution, in order to adopt it, you and your friends/colleagues setting up the charity need to sign and date it. In so doing, you are becoming the trustees of the charity until the first annual general meeting.

We will go into more depth in Chapter 5 about the role of the trustees, but in essence, a trustee is responsible for the money that other people have given to the charity and they must ensure that it is spent on the stated cause and correctly accounted for. The legal definition of a trustee is those people who are responsible for 'the general control and management of the administration of a charity', so you do not want to appoint your first trustees lightly.

Ideally, you are looking at setting up with at least three trustees. There is in fact no limit on the number of trustees you can have but, in reality, if you have too many, decision making becomes unwieldy and unproductive. You want trustees whose skills can contribute to the effective running of the organization, and that should ultimately be what dictates the number.

Now you have completed your constitution and you have become a charity, you can apply directly to Her Majesty's Revenue and Customs (HMRC) for tax relief and advice on claiming gift aid. They will issue you with an HMRC charity number which should be accepted by banks and grant funders as evidence of your charitable status instead of a registered charity number.

As a small charity according to charity law, you can call yourself a charity but you must be careful how you present yourself to potential funders, donors or the public. Never use the words 'registered' or 'charity status' but you can say something along the lines of 'our charity is a not-for-profit organization recognized as charitable by HMRC for tax purposes'. Don't actually quote the HMRC number as this could leave your charity open to fraudulent activity.

Remember this: Scale of project

When trying to decide the structure that best suits your ambitions, it is worth asking yourself, 'How big is the need you are trying to address?' Are you talking about a local, regional, national or international scale? And how long will your charity be needed? If it is a response to a specific disaster, for example, it will not need to be established for a great length of time.

Remember this: Terminology

An individual charity's purposes can also be called its 'aims' or sometimes its 'objects'. Whichever term you choose to use, your aims are usually expressed in the objects clause of your governing document or constitution.

▶ Opening a bank account

Although you are not a registered charity, you can still open a bank account in your charity name. In the main, your governing document and an HMRC number is enough, but some banks insist on a registration number. If you are having difficulties, it might be worth approaching one of the specialist charity banks such as Charities Aid Foundation (CAF) Bank, Charity Bank or Unity Trust Bank, who are sometimes more understanding than the high street banks.

If all else fails and it is not possible to register a bank account in the charity name, you could decide to open a personal account in the treasurer's name, making sure that it is separate from any other personal accounts s/he may have. This is not an ideal scenario but, if needs must, then make a written statement to the other trustees to the effect that the treasurer holds money in Account X on behalf of the charity, and try to organize the need for two signatures to sign cheques from that account. Keep in mind that the easiest way to fall foul of regulation and fall out with your friends/founder/trustees is to get the money wrong.

Remember this

When you open your bank account(s), remember to ask for a meeting with a member of the bank's charity/not-for-profit department, even if they work at a different branch. More and more banks now have dedicated teams dealing with charities and it's important that you get to know your local representative as soon as you can.

Try it now

It is worth researching which high street and charity banks will accept a governing document (constitution) or HMRC number when registering a charity bank account rather than a Charity Commission registered number. Once you've whittled it down, you can then look at who offers the best rates. Do this well in advance of any fundraising activities if you want to avoid the problem of how to bank donations.

BIGGER CHARITIES

Bigger charities that want or need to register with the Charity Commission have to go through the same set-up processes as a small charity: deciding on a name, working out ways to raise money and achieve its aims, and recruiting trustees to run the charity. However, rather than having a constitution, bigger charities require different sorts of governing documents.

▶ Types of governing documents

There are three main types of governing document and, once you have chosen the type of organization that best fits your needs, you then choose whichever type of document that fits your charity. The three main types of governing document are:

1 Constitution – much like that used by smaller unregistered charities, a constitution or rules is best suited to charitable associations.

2 Trust Deed – this is the governing document required for charitable trusts.

3 Articles of Association – this is the appropriate governing document for a charitable company.

You can find model forms for all of these types of governing documents on the Charity Commission website. Once you have downloaded the appropriate model, you simply fill in the objects (purposes) of your specific charity, and a few other clauses where options are available.

Another way of getting model governing documents is to become a member of The Charity Law Association (CLA) which produces such models free of charge for members. It costs around £45 for a charity (up to three members) to join or £50 for an individual, but there are other advantages of membership such as free quarterly meetings with speakers and networking opportunities.

Alternatively, as we saw with the small charities, if your organization is associated with one of the large national charities that produces an approved governing document, such as the scouts and guides, the Women's Institute, Playing Fields Association, Amateur Sports Clubs and many more, then you can approach them directly for a model governing document. The advantage of using documents from these 'umbrella' charities is that they come already furnished with agreed objects and administrative provisions that are specific to that particular type of organization.

Choosing a name

Choosing a memorable and fitting name for your charity might seem pretty straightforward, but you'd be surprised at just how tricky it can be. First of all, you want something eye-catching that the public will remember, but it should also give them some idea of what your charity is about. Given that your charity name will appear on all of your fundraising campaign and appeal literature, you want it to be good and look good. The dilemma is that with 180,000 charities already registered, getting something original, catchy and informative that is not too close to any existing charity names is something of a challenge.

One of the things ascribed to the great success of the military charity, Help for Heroes, is its emotive name. Somehow this title caught the zeitgeist and the national mood. You would be hard pressed to find a name as successful as this one, but it is not impossible.

Just bear in mind that, legally, a charity name must not include any word or expression which might cause offence and that it must not be identical or too similar too any other names on the Charity Commission Register if your charity is to be accepted for registration.

It is a good idea therefore before you go through the rigmarole of executing a governing document, etc., that you check the Register of Charities online with regard to the availability or suitability of names. I would also recommend that you do an internet search for your proposed name, just in case there is an unregistered charity or non-charitable company using that name in your area, or in the country.

Once you have decided on a name, there is just one more check before you register it with the appropriate body or bodies. Make sure you can also reserve or register your chosen name as a domain name on the internet, even if you do not plan an immediate online presence. You would feel rather foolish if you went through the whole registration process, only to find that a commercial company halfway around the world had bought up the domain name that fits your charity.

Remember this: Legal name

Even if you register your charity and the name appears on the Register, under the general law, you do not have any rights to the name. You can of course register the name at Companies House if you are incorporated, or you could register it as a trademark which confers some legal protection.

Charity trustees

There will be a more in-depth look at the role of trustees in Chapter 4, but here is a brief overview. All charities, irrespective of size and type, must have a body of trustees who are responsible for the control and management of the administration of the charity – they check that those who actually run the charity are doing a good job, if you like.

If your organization is set up with a constitution or rules, then the charity trustees will probably be called executive or management committee members but they perform the same role as trustees, just as the directors of charitable companies will do.

Being a charity trustee is a time-consuming and far-reaching post and anyone agreeing to become a trustee should be made fully aware of the commitment needed to carry out their responsibilities. When forming your trustee board, you are looking for candidates who can bring a broad spectrum of relevant experience and skills to the table. You want trustees whose various talents complement one another and, if possible, whose experience is garnered from a diverse range of social and economic backgrounds. In addition, you want people who are prepared to get involved in the charity and who will take an active part either by being hands-on or by supporting staff, if you have them.

Anyone over the age of 18 can become a charity trustee, with a few legal and common-sense exceptions. Namely, there cannot be a conflict of interests between a trustee's duties and their personal interests, they cannot have a criminal record involving deception or dishonesty, or have been a bankrupt or previously disqualified as a company director or charity trustee.

Finally, being a trustee is generally a labour of love, as they are not supposed to benefit financially from being a trustee, unless specifically authorized to do so by the charity's governing documents. In my experience, the vast majority of trustees give of their time selflessly and generously, only accepting recompense for out-of-pocket expenses. Being a trustee is an important and essential role, as we'll see in Chapter 5, and one that requires dedication, purpose and energy without looking for financial reward.

Remember this: Best of both worlds

Many charities set up a subsidiary trading company that is limited by guarantee. This subsidiary then gifts its profits back to the parent charity. In this way, the parent charity is protected from any undue financial risks from its trading venture. It also has the advantage of keeping all trading activities clearly distinct from its fundraising and its core activities and those determined by the charity's object.

I have run a number of trading companies alongside the charity over the years, one delivering training developed in the first instance for the charity's own staff team. It is important that both charity and trading company stand alone – separate accounts, separate directors, etc., and NEVER use charity funds to prop up a poorly performing trading company.

Try it now

If you are setting up a charity that works with children and/or vulnerable adults, not only do you need a suitable child or vulnerable adults protection policy, but clearly it behoves you to make the appropriate checks on trustees as well as employees.

Remember this: Choose wisely

It's often tempting to appoint trustees because of their status or position in the community, but that is the role of a patron or president of the charity. To be a successful trustee, a person must bring more than just status to the role.

Case study: Jonny Wineberg, Community Futures Trust CIC

The Newsite Community Project on a deprived estate in Newville started as three local parents running a street party in the summer of 2012. With its success, they decided that they wanted to do something more substantial for their children and to improve community relationships.

With advice from their local voluntary sector support group, Newville Voluntary Action (NVA), they recognized that it was important to start by identifying the issues facing the community, with the community. A meeting was held at the local church, with a facilitator and 40 local people aged from 10 to 80 attending. In six workshop groups, they were asked to answer:

* What are the two most important issues for the community?
* What can a new organization, either directly or indirectly, do to address these issues?
* What resources will be needed to address these issues?
* Who will need to be involved in such a project to address these issues?
* What results will such a project need to achieve for it to be deemed a success?

The groups fed back and identified unemployment, crime, lack of prospects, poor health and drugs as priority issues to be addressed. The group then came up with two key purposes for their project:

* To give the next generation the best chance in life possible
* To create a strong community where people supported each other and made the Newsite Estate an enjoyable place to live.

After discussion in groups, it was agreed that two approaches should be taken to address these.

The Newsite Community Project would focus on developing as a Childcare and Play provision. The daytime childcare would help parents to access employment and training and, combined with the play provision, would help children's development to improve their prospects.

The local Residents Association would be revived to develop more community activities and promote healthy living. The two groups would work together to get parenting training delivered and a new parents' support group. They would also conduct a community survey to get more evidence of need for the work they wanted to deliver. This was for three reasons:

- so that they would be sure that they were undertaking the right work
- so that local people felt involved
- to have evidence for funders.

Eight people agreed to start a committee as The Newsite Community Project and five others agreed to join the Residents' Association. Two of the three original parents wanted to be on both. Over the next two months, the Community Project met every other week. NVA helped them draft a constitution and, with that in place, they opened a bank account. This meant that they could start to bid for funding. It was agreed that, once they were more established, they would apply to become a registered charity but they could function as a voluntary group for the first year.

Both groups developed clear and measurable objectives for their first year and were supported to develop action plans to show how they would accomplish these. These included the actions to be taken; who was responsible for each action; the resources they would need – human, financial, equipment, materials and venues – and how they would show they had achieved their objectives (evaluation). They fostered links with their local council, who helped them gather additional evidence of need from statistics on deprivation, education and health that they had.

With plans in place, bids were put in to the local Community Foundation, the local council's Early Years fund and the Lottery's Awards for All programme to fund the survey, some play equipment, weekly play sessions, a parenting course and a summer play week, with a community day. All these were written with local people involved, with the play sessions, where possible, described by the children.

Over the next year, with the success of these funding bids, the needs survey was completed, and the Community Project began to look at bidding to fund permanent staff. Links were made with Play England and the need to register with Ofsted was identified and work started to reach their standards.

This case study is based on practice described in: Wineberg, J., 'Time to Transform Our Communities', www.timetotoc.org.uk, Commitment in Communities, Manchester 2006.

Focus points

Firstly, decide what type of charity organization would best fit the size, style and aims of your set-up.

If you are staying small, use a model constitution for your charity; these model forms are available online.

If you are a bigger charity or considering changing your status, you can still download model samples of governing documents for your charity online.

Choose the name of your charity with careful consideration and only after checking out what names are already in use.

With or without Charity Commission registration, you need to set up a bank account in the name of the charity, wherever possible.

Appoint your charity trustees with a view to what skills and talents they can bring to the organization.

Next step

Now you are ready to think about registering your charity, if appropriate, and in the next chapter, we'll look at the various steps you need to take to ensure successful registration.

3

Registering a charity

In this chapter, you will learn:

- ▶ *About the benefits of registering as a charity*
- ▶ *What the registration process involves*
- ▶ *About the documentation requirements*
- ▶ *Who is exempt from registration*

As you have seen from the previous chapters, there is quite a lot to do before you can think about registering as a charity. It may well be that you have operated as a small charitable organization (with an income of less than £5,000) for some time and your organization has been so successful and the income has grown so much that you must now register.

Alternatively, you may want to register as a charity from the outset. So, once you have established that this is the right path for your venture, and you have identified your charitable purpose (aims) and who is going to benefit, plus you've found some people prepared to be trustees of your charity, you are ready to begin the procedure of registering your charity with the Charity Commission for England and Wales.

Since the law governing charities is slightly different in Scotland and Northern Ireland, the advice and procedure for registering a charity in those regions differs from the advice given here and on the Charity Commission website. If you are setting up a charity in Scotland or Northern Ireland, I recommend that you to check out the website of the Office of the Scottish Charity Regulator (OSCR) – www.oscr.org.uk, and that of the Charity Commission for Northern Ireland (CCNI) – www. charitycommissionni.org.uk, where you will find specific details for registering a charity in that region.

In reality, you effectively have to set up the charity (adopt charitable objects) and get key players in place before you apply for your charity to be registered – and this is where those who have operated as a small charitable organization for some time have the edge because they will already have formally adopted a governing document at their inception.

Only once you have all this information in place will you be able to answer all the questions and legal requirements of the Charity Commission. The good news is that you can still claim tax exemption from the moment that your organization started to carry out exclusively charitable aims, rather than the date of registration, so this time setting up is not wasted in terms of financial benefit.

Why register?

Given that many small organizations with an income of less than £5,000 enjoy charitable status without being a registered charity, you might well wonder if it is worth the hassle of registering.

Well, that is a fair question, so let me point out some of the advantages of being a registered charity:

▶ If you are thinking of applying to trusts or state bodies for funding, you are more likely to be awarded a grant if you are a registered charity.

▶ Charities are not required to pay Corporation Tax or Stamp Duty Tax.

▶ As a registered charity, you are able to reclaim gift aid on donations and you can benefit from the Give As You Earn scheme. These tax-efficient measures are not available to non-registered organizations.

▶ The buildings that you use for your charitable purposes as a registered charity may attract up to 80 per cent relief on normal business rates.

▶ Sometimes you can get reductions on VAT as a registered charity.

▶ All gifts received by the charity are free from Inheritance Tax.

▶ Finally, a registered charity number lends credibility to your organization. Donors and supporters are more likely to have confidence in a registered charity, especially if the work you undertake is in a distant land, and this can be reflected in their donations.

Remember this

Before you can register, you must have a bank account in the name of the charity – not your own name – and bank statements must show that you have had at least £5,000 turnover in the last 12 months.

Try it now

Don't let red tape stand in the way of your fundraising. If you haven't yet registered, you can still get fundraising – invite people to donate to your cause but make sure you tell them that the money is being used to achieve your charitable objects, and it will help you to register as a charity. Bear in mind that it has to be a donation, rather than a loan.

Applying for registration

The only way you can apply for registration is through the Charity Commission's online application service. It is easy to use and there is plenty of online help to guide you through the process. Once you have filled in your details on the first six screens, you will receive a reference number, which means that you can then save the form and return to it at any time, which takes the pressure off a little.

WHAT DO YOU NEED?

Before you start the online application, you need to have a name for your charity and you need to be clear in your own head and on paper about what your organization does and the way that it does it, as this will come up on the questionnaire. You also need to be armed with the names, addresses and dates of birth of all of the trustees. Finally, you need the governing document and signed trustee declaration in PDF format plus bank statements showing a gross income of £5,000 to attach to the application form when you submit it. If your organization is a company, you will need a Certificate of Incorporation (see Chapter 2) in addition.

When forming its judgement about whether your organization can be registered as a charity or not, the Charity Commission takes into account three things, as outlined on their website:

▶ **Aims**

What your organization's aims are, whether those aims are charitable and whether the aims are fully and accurately reflected in your stated objects. Generally speaking, aims (purposes) are not charitable if they are for the benefit of a named person or specific individual, for example. In effect, your charity aims must fall within, or be comparable to the legal description of charitable purpose, as set out in the Charities Act. These descriptions are as follows:

- the prevention or relief of poverty;

- the advancement of education;

- the advancement of religion;

- the advancement of health or the saving of lives;

- the advancement of citizenship or community development;

- the advancement of the arts, culture, heritage or science;

- the advancement of amateur sport;

- the advancement of human rights, conflict resolution or reconciliation or the promotion of religious or racial harmony or equality and diversity;

- the advancement of environmental protection or improvement;

- the relief of those in need, by reason of youth, age, ill-health, disability, financial hardship or other disadvantage;

- the advancement of animal welfare;

- the promotion of the efficiency of the armed forces of the Crown, or of the efficiency of the police, fire and rescue services or ambulance services;

- other purposes currently recognized as charitable and any new charitable purposes which are similar to another charitable purpose.

Benefit

There must be an identifiable benefit or benefits. So it must be clear what the benefits are and how they relate to the aims of your charity. Any benefits you claim should be weighed against any possible detriment or harm.

Public benefit

Benefit must be to the public or a section of the public (not too restricted). For example, a local village hall could be shown to benefit the residents of that village and the surrounding inhabitants; medical research into multiple sclerosis could be shown to benefit sufferers of multiple sclerosis; and an organization devoted to the conservation of an endangered species such as the white rhino could be shown to benefit humanity in general.

You must make sure that you satisfy all three of these requirements if your charity is to be successful in its application for registration.

Remember this: What's in a name?

As we saw in the previous chapter, when deciding what you will call your charity, it cannot be too close to or the same as a charity name already on the Register. It's worth investing a little time in scrutinizing the Register of Charities to make sure that your chosen name is not already taken, as it will result in your application being rejected by the Charity Commission, if the name is taken or it is too close to an existing name.

Try it now

All supporting documentation for your registration application, i.e. your governing document and signed trustee declarations, must be submitted as PDF files. Have a go at creating PDF files now – most modern scanners offer the option to save files in a PDF format. Also, if you are using more recent versions of Word or an equivalent, you can save documents in PDF format. If all else fails, you can convert most documents to PDF by using free online or downloadable software, such as PrimoPDF or CutePDF, or you could buy Adobe Acrobat software. Have a play and see what works best for you.

WHEN WILL WE HEAR?

The Charity Commission aims to give you an initial response to your application within 15 working days, but on average it takes about 30 days to successfully register an application. Bear in mind that the Charity Commission is primarily the sector regulator, and as such, it is extremely busy. So if you need your organization to be registered by a particular date, it is wise to submit your application in good time.

Occasionally, the Commission has further questions that it wants answered before it can give a final decision. If this is the case you will be contacted for further information or clarification.

If your application is successful, your organization will be entered on the Register of Charities, and details about your charity will appear on the Public Register within two working days of being accepted. As well as the nominated correspondent of the charity, each trustee will also receive a letter and a booklet welcoming them to trusteeship and confirming the successful registration.

Once your charity has been registered, you or someone within the organization is then required to:

▶ Keep the accounts

▶ Inform the Charity Commission of any changes to your governing document

▶ Inform the Charity Commission of any changes in the details of your charity as shown on the Register, such as a change of address

▶ Inform the Charity Commission if the charity ceases operating.

In addition, if your charity has a gross income exceeding £10,000 a year, you must send back the annual return duly completed to the Charity Commission. If your gross income exceeds £25,000 – which is good going – then you need additionally to send the accounts, examiner's or auditor's report and trustees' annual report within ten months of the end of your financial year.

Remember this: Speeding up the process

Granting charitable status as a registered charity is a complex legal process that takes time but the whole thing can be speeded up significantly if you use an approved governing document (with permission from the umbrella body, if applicable), if you have supplied all the required documentation in the relevant format and if you have completed the sections on the online application form in full. Then, if you still haven't heard within four weeks of submission, you should chase it up.

FAILED APPLICATIONS

If after considering your application, the Charity Commission decides that your organization is not exclusively charitable, that is, it doesn't satisfy the three Aims, Benefits and Public Benefit criteria, they will write and let you know. You will of course have an opportunity to contest their decision and, if you disagree, you should write setting out the reasons. They will then review their decision. Irrespective of whether or not the Charity Commission accepts your appeal or not, you still have the right of appeal to the Charity Tribunal.

Some of the more common reasons for rejection are when the aims of the organization may appear at first glance to be charitable but in fact are not. For example, sports clubs that only benefit their members or sporting excellence as opposed to facilities open for the benefit of all or specific groups such as the elderly; organizations created for political aims; aims which mean that those running the organization stand to significantly benefit personally; international friendship organizations such as town twinning associations, and this may seem obvious, but worth pointing out nonetheless, if the aims are illegal. If your charity falls into any of those categories, I'm afraid your application will not be successful.

Case study: Church of the Holy Nativity

Holy Nativity is the parish church of Chapel House in the west of Newcastle-upon-Tyne. We are a relatively small parish in terms of population.

We serve an area with significant hidden needs, including a high proportion of older residents and also carers. The church hosts and co-ordinates a variety of community initiatives to lend support to people of all ages, most especially people who live with health difficulties such as dementia.

Like most Church of England parish churches, it began and grew without being registered with the Charities Commission. Parish churches in England are established in law, so they are not generally required to register (though exceptions exist). Canon Law requires each parish church to elect church wardens and a Parochial Church Council (PCC).

The PCC undertakes to hold public Annual Parochial Church Meetings and formal elections, to record minutes of all meetings and to present accounts which are checked and signed by an independent examiner, many of whom give their services free or for a nominal sum.

For 45 years Holy Nativity operated successfully under this system, with minimal administrative costs and relatively straightforward management procedures. Over time, the old church hall had to be closed and the church faced urgent significant repairs and refurbishment. The parish launched a 'Community Project' to make the church accessible and multi-functional and to build essential new facilities to help serve the identified needs in the local community. The project grew considerably in the making and had to raise funds to the total of £900,000. BIG Lottery and several charitable trusts provided £700,000 and local fundraising brought in £200,000.

The project grant income placed Holy Nativity in a new category with regard to the Charities Commission. At that time (2007), any parish church with an annual income of over £100,000 was required to register formally. We could have applied for an exemption on the grounds that the income was not a regular annual income and would be used in capital development. However, we were also advised of plans to reduce the threshold income to £50,000. We estimated that the financial turnover of our community project could possibly extend our annual income to that level. We decided to register the church with the Charities Commission.

Many pages of detailed personal and corporate information had to be disclosed and papers signed and submitted by all elected representatives, now formally 'trustees'. The long and detailed legal responsibilities sent to each member raised considerable concern and only the reassuring intervention of the Diocesan Secretary persuaded some members against resigning. It was sobering to realize the high level of accountability we now faced. In a sense, there was no change in our legal standing, though it seemed as if we were now taking on a much bigger responsibility.

The production of the new annual report is now a mammoth task. The pre-registration ten-page booklet with brief reports from activities groups and simple accounts gave way to the new 34-page annual report and accounts which gives details of organizational structure, governance and management, objectives and outcomes, policies and plans, all in 'formal' terminology, and which now makes our activities sound overwhelmingly complicated.

The accounts have to be fully audited – an obligation which adds nearly £3,000 to our annual expenditure. The auditors translate our bookkeeping into 12 pages of multi-column figures. And, we are assured that all the accountancy firms in the world will be able to measure our transparent accounts. Meanwhile, the only people really interested – the people who live here – rely on the treasurer to provide a simple summary of the monthly income and expenditure so we can accept ownership and agree budgets.

Being a 'registered' charity offers a reasonable guarantee to others that we are a charity with acceptable aims and practices. It is arguably easier to attract grants from potential funding organizations, though most funders recognize (and can check) the status of a parish church regardless of registration. Registration has made us more 'professional' and has led us on some steep learning curves regarding the use of computer technology, administration, accounting and management.

In reality we remain a modest group of volunteers who enjoy getting on with planning events through the church's year and welcoming visitors. In the background a small team of administrators devote much more time than previously to managing the project and maintaining the building.

So long as new volunteers keep joining the team, this church and its community projects have a future. Like all charities, survival also depends on free-will giving, an increasing proportion of which may be needed for the employment of people with essential skills.

Focus points

Registering as a charity offers some financial benefits and a degree of protection for trustees and staff.

Before registering, you must establish your Aims (purposes), Benefit and Public Benefit and ensure they are charitable.

Be sure your charity name is original if you want to avoid rejection of your application.

You must apply online for charity registration with all supporting documents in pdf format.

You should hear a decision within about a month, although the Charity Commission may have queries that need to be answered before a final decision can be made, and this tends to delay the process.

If you fail in your application, you can appeal. Alternatively, you may wish to review your application, make adjustments and then reapply.

Next step

Whether you've gone down the route of becoming a registered charity or you've stayed as a small charitable organization, you still need a good team of people working together for your cause. So let's take a look at the executive and non-executive roles that need to be filled.

4

Management and governance

In this chapter you will learn:

▶ *Who runs a charity – key roles within the organization*

▶ *What the difference is between good management and good governance*

▶ *About enrolling volunteers*

▶ *How to recruit trustees and board members*

▶ *How to work on strategy and governance with a volunteer board*

All fledgling organizations need a structure and a group of people to run them. Giving some forethought to how you set up the structure of your charity – and your role within it – could determine how smoothly it runs in the future.

Within the organization, you are looking at a team of people who will run the charity on a day-to-day basis, namely the management, also known as the executive; and a group of volunteers who are responsible for making sure the charity is delivering to its object, is well-run, efficient and safe, namely the trustees, also known as the non-executive.

Remember this

For the purposes of this chapter, the people who form the governing body of a charity are known as trustees. However, in the wider world, trustees can also be known as directors, board members, non-executive directors, governors or committee members. Essentially, their role is the same.

Choosing the right structure

When you are starting from scratch, it is often the executive members of the team that are put in place first. So, that is someone or several people to deliver your service to your charity's beneficiaries – those who are at the coal-face, so to speak, directly helping the people or the causes that got you fired-up in the first place. You will probably also put a lot of emphasis on the team of people who are devoted to fundraising – whether these are members of staff or volunteers. And then you clearly need a management team for the operational running and delivery, and to run the support function of the financial and administrative aspects of the operation. Together, they form the team that implements the strategic plan.

Clearly, you have to have the right people in the right jobs so that the organization, however big or small, runs effectively and efficiently. With the best will in the world, even if you plan a sensible structure, it is usually a bit haphazard in the early days, with a few core people trying to fulfil many of the aforementioned functions, and responding to incidents and events as they happen. Nonetheless, as the dust settles on your new venture, with the right structure in place for your service delivery and its management, you should be in good shape to take the charity forward.

Even while you are still at the early, plate-spinning stage of your charity's growth, it is important that you give some consideration to how, as the founder, you see your position and personal aims within the organization. Bear in mind that those who have the creative drive, focus and charisma to start an organization often lack the attention to detail and application needed to manage and grow the charity in the long term. Clearly, this is not always a given, but it's often the case in the small charities that I have encountered over the years, and a balance of skills is needed.

If you recognize yourself in this scenario, then you need to make sure the structure of your charity is such that the organization does not grind to a halt without you and, sooner or later, you should give some thought to your own exit strategy – not from the organization altogether necessarily, but from being the lynchpin of it. Perhaps, once the charity is established, you could move into a governance or ambassadorial role, whereby you are still intrinsically involved but it is less time-consuming and hands-on. At the opposite end of the spectrum, you may wish to leave the management of the charity to those with the appropriate mix of skills, while you devote your talents to helping the beneficiaries of the charity – going back to being a frontline service provider.

Initially, as the founder, you will almost certainly be fulfilling one or more of the functions of the executive, whether you like it or not. However, there comes a time when you can and should decide which role you want to do. Some founders opt to be the chair of the board of trustees so they can oversee the effective running of the charity. Some opt to be the chief executive, so that they can steer the running of the organization and retain control of their vision. And a few are happier getting back to basics, delivering the goods and working directly with the beneficiaries – although rarely are they happy to relinquish control completely, unless to someone who they feel shares their ideals and thoughts about the way forward.

The problem comes when the founder insists on continuing to fulfil all of those functions or one they are not skilled or suited to do, possibly because they don't trust anyone else to do the job right. If that sounds familiar, then perhaps you need to take a step back and decide where your strengths lie, and then focus in that particular area while appointing someone else with the skills to take on the other responsibilities.

The 'honest brokerage' between executives and non-executives is crucial to ensuring people with the right skills take on the right roles and responsibilities.

VOLUNTEERS

While sorting out your executive team and staff, do not underestimate the value of using volunteers in the organization, especially while there is more work to be done than there are people to do it all. In fact, many start-up and fledgling charities would not survive the journey to self-sufficiency without the help of volunteers, and plenty if not most well-established charities run smoothly only because of the invaluable contribution made by the volunteers who augment the skills and efforts of the paid staff.

Of course, there are certain risks involved with counting on the services of volunteers, and we will go into more details on this in Chapter 9 when we look at team dynamics. For now though, let us agree that volunteers are useful notably because they cost very little – it's customary to pay expenses – but also because they are clearly committed to your cause and they can bring skills to the organization that you may not otherwise be able to afford – don't fall into the trap of thinking volunteers are only useful for basic frontline tasks; there are professionals out there who are keen to volunteer their expertise too. In the past, I have had a professional recruitment consultant and a Harvard Professor who have offered their voluntary support.

The other great thing about volunteers, interns and work-placement students is that, if they prove themselves to be useful, they are ideal candidates to recruit when you are looking to create or fill a paid staff job.

Good governance

Received wisdom on the ideal structure for a charity is that a board of trustees or directors takes on responsibility for the general governance, and an overall legal and financial view of the charity. The chair of the board of trustees appoints a chief executive or managing director who is responsible for the general running of the organization. In turn, the chief executive then appoints an executive team and staff to carry out the essential executive functions of the charity, in accordance with the policies approved by the board.

In reality, the procedure is usually completely about-face. What usually happens in practice is that the enthusiastic founder of the charity appoints him or herself as chief executive and gets a team of willing staff/volunteers around them to deliver services. Then s/he appoints the first board of trustees. Now there is nothing intrinsically wrong with doing it this way around but it does have inherent pitfalls.

Firstly, the danger of the founder appointing the board of trustees is that it can then be difficult for the new trustees to challenge a strong-willed founder, and they can end up simply 'rubber-stamping' all the decisions and directions proposed by the founder/chief executive.

In fact, what is needed from the board is a degree of objective accountability – and that's not impossible, but not that easy when a trustee is potentially challenging the vision and authority of the charity's single-minded, visionary leader and founder – who incidentally invited the trustee onto the board in the first place.

So let's take a look at what the proper role of a trustee might entail and then how you go about appointing trustees.

Remember this: Forever in charge

As the founder, even if you decide the role for you within the organization is not as chairman of the board of trustees or chief executive, but being involved in frontline services or taking another back-seat role, don't be surprised if people still seek your opinion or defer to your views. This can undermine the authority of the person appointed to manage the charity, and you will have to be sensitive to the situation.

Remember this: Inspiration

The list of responsibilities for a trustee is long but one duty that is often overlooked is the need to occasionally remind everyone why they got involved in this work in the first place and about the mission that they all share. The value of being able to inspire and motivate the executive and other board members to work well should not be underestimated.

WHAT IS THE ROLE OF A TRUSTEE?

When you agree to be a charity trustee, you agree to take on the responsibility and to an extent the liability, along with the other members of the board, for ensuring the delivery of the mission and administration of the charity. You have duties and responsibilities to the charity, its beneficiaries and its supporters.

Trustees come from all sorts of different walks of life but what unifies them is the desire to offer their skills, knowledge and enthusiasm for the benefit of the charity. The vast majority of trustees are volunteers – some of the larger charities offer paid trustee positions but this is rare, and most trustees only receive reasonable out-of-pocket expenses that they incur while working on behalf of the charity.

As a trustee, your duties include making sure the charity is well-run and efficient (duty of care), which will bring you into contact with senior staff, with particular responsibility for appointing, managing and supporting the chief executive. You also have to make sure that the charity looks after and uses its money prudently (duty of prudence) and that it follows the law governing how it raises and uses funds. The board of trustees is obliged to ensure that their charity complies with charity law and any other legal requirements, so it is important that you keep up to speed with developments within the charity and legal sector. However, first and foremost, as a board and working together, you must make sure that the management of the charity is operating in such a way as to fulfil the charity's purpose and objects, as set out in its governing documents, so that it continues to benefit the public for whom it was set up. The degree to which the board of trustees are involved in the strategic planning of the charity varies from organization to organization. Of course, trustees can also help with fundraising – especially in terms of introductions – but their primary role is governance.

Within the board, there are two key roles, namely that of chair and treasurer, which represent special responsibilities. The chair of the board of trustees has a close working relationship with the chief executive officer, and the treasurer is responsible for the written accounts, and naturally works closely with the finance director of the organization.

The size of the board differs in every organization, and ultimately it is not written in stone. On a practical note, you need enough members to offer the essential skills and experience that you require. If you go for a small board, it can be easier to manage but it can pose problems in terms of reaching a quorum for important decision making if one of the board or a member is absent. Conversely, a large board can be unwieldy and meetings become ineffective if every member wants to have their say. In many ways, the size is not what counts – it is the composition that it most important. Get that right and you will have a good board that will help to take the organization forward.

Although being a trustee is a serious undertaking and can be hard work, especially in the formative years of a charity's existence, it can also be immensely rewarding and not only should it offer a chance to make a positive difference but also to add to your own skills set and experience.

There isn't a charity in existence that does not owe a huge debt of gratitude to its trustees. Without great trustees and chairs, I would never have become a charity chief executive.

Try it now

Before signing up to be a trustee, you should make sure you find out as much as possible about what the charity does and what will be expected of you. Also check what your levels of liability are (see Chapter 11). You can then make an informed decision about whether or not you can devote enough time to do things properly and whether or not your skills and experience can help this particular charity.

Remember this: Integrity

Sometimes a trustee may be invited to become a member of the board of trustees on another charity at the same time. This is allowed but it is the responsibility of that trustee to make sure that they have no personal conflicts of interest.

Remember this: Board development

The qualities of the founding members of a board focus on getting the nascent charity established and set-up to run effectively. It is not for the faint-hearted or prima donnas. As the organization grows, so the role of the board members needs to develop also. You might want to consider expanding the board's membership, or you might prefer to find replacements as founding members step aside, but you will be looking for new members who can meet the specific needs of the expanding organization.

APPOINTING A TRUSTEE

Anyone over the age of 18 can be a trustee of an unincorporated charity (the age is 16 for an incorporated charity). How trustees are appointed is usually set out in the governing document for the charity. As a generality, new trustees are appointed by the existing trustees, and are recruited either by word of mouth or by advertisement. However, at the beginning, it is more often the chief executive and/or founder who chooses the board. As the charity develops, so formalized procedures will be developed whereby the trustees will recruit to the board themselves.

▶ Finding trustees

It is not easy to find the right people who have useful skills, who can plan strategically and who are willing to devote the necessary time, energy and heart to your cause, but don't compromise on what you are looking for. All too often, friends, family and supporters are appointed as trustees in the hope that enthusiasm alone will carry the day. This is often a mistake.

I have had the privilege of working closely as a CEO with some excellent chairs and dedicated, efficient trustees. But I have also seen the damage that incompetent members of the board and weak chairs can inflict on an organization, and it is devastating.

So persevere in your search, identify which skills your board needs and interview people until you find the right ones. Get trustees with relevant experience and passion, and a chair who will govern his or her board with strong, dedicated leadership. After all, the buck ultimately stops with the trustees – although the management runs the organization, they are the ones who have to take responsibility if something goes wrong.

▶ Parting company

Once appointed, there is no set period of time that you serve as a trustee. Some charities stipulate how long you can be a trustee in their governing document, and this can be a wise precaution as there are occasions when a trustee does not work out well, for whatever reasons, and if that time proviso is set out in the governing document, then you are able to let the trustee go graciously by not offering re-election. Often trustees want to serve a credible time and then offer their experience to another charity.

By the same token, if a trustee wants to stop being on the board of the charity, they can resign or retire at any time, but there are occasionally legal requirements governing this, especially in the case of unincorporated charities.

The problem comes when the board and/or executive feel that a trustee is disruptive, behaving badly – bullying, aggressive, rude or arrogant, lazy, ineffective or simply no longer adding value to the board. If this behaviour continues after it has been pointed out to the individual concerned, then it falls to the chair of the board of trustees, as diplomatically as possible and in private, to suggest that this trustee's skills might be better used elsewhere and now might be a good time to move on. Most people will accept graciously rather than stay on a board where they are not particularly welcome – after all, they are volunteering their services – but this is not always the case, especially if they feel that it comes down to a clash of personality with another member or the executive. In the worst case scenario, where a trustee declines to leave, the only option is to vote them off theb board, but this is unpleasant for all concerned and can have ramifications in terms of the organization's reputation.

A way to avoid or address bad or ineffectual trustee behaviour is to have a code of good governance in place and then the board, perhaps together with the senior management, can work through it as a group so such problems can be addressed without individuals being singled out for blame.

On a happier note, I should point out that such situations are rare, and most trustees devote many years of loyal service to the charities they embrace.

Remember this: Passion

Even if you can offer skills to a board that will make a significant contribution, you should only agree to become a trustee if you feel passionate about the cause. I say this because the duties of a trustee can be time-consuming and sometimes onerous, board meetings are a lengthy process, and you will only enjoy being involved if you care deeply about the end results.

Try it now

Review the last few meetings of the board of trustees. How much time was spent deliberating decisions that ultimately should be the responsibility of the executive? For example, the details of how the budget was allocated rather than did the team accomplish the goals by using the budget effectively? Make sure the lines between what is the responsibility of the board and what is the responsibility of the executive do not become blurred. It will save time and heartache for everyone in the long run.

Remember this: Defunct

Each board member has a role to fulfil and a contribution to make. If a trustee is too pliable, apathetic or subversive behind the scenes, their role is in effect defunct. Sadly, passive behaviour is often harder to address than open aggressive behaviour but it is just as dangerous and damaging to the board and charity and, although it is harder to bring into the open, it needs to be resolved.

EXECUTIVE AND NON-EXECUTIVE RELATIONS

According to the Association of Chief Executives of Voluntary Organizations (ACEVO), the relationship between a charity CEO and his or her board is crucial to the effective running of the charity, but tensions can quickly rise, especially in challenging economic times.

In my experience, the relationship between a CEO and their chair in particular needs to be especially strong and resilient, and based on mutual trust. For that to happen there must be good communication. All too often, the CEO and his/ her executive are not on the same page as the board, and expectations and attitudes can differ, especially about the thorny issue of impact reporting and measuring outcomes, for example. Developing open communication and trust is crucial.

Case study: Janet Thornton, Trustee of ACRE (Action with Communities in Rural England), Rural Action Yorkshire and Involve Yorkshire and Humber (co-Vice Chair)

I had been actively involved in village activities since I became a stay-at-home mum and over the following 15 years my involvement in various local organizations, activities and events had kept me occupied and proactive within my community, but they were not particularly intellectually challenging. I was bored and needed a fresh challenge. As I was still committed to volunteering, becoming a trustee was appealing, particularly as the opportunities to get back into the job market in an interesting part-time role were extremely limited.

Sitting on a trustee board involves lots of paperwork and reports to read and requires you to sit in meetings for two to three hours at a time (or longer!). It only appeals to a certain type of person.

I studied Business Studies in my further education, so I felt reasonably comfortable with the financial scrutiny work involved – I knew my way around a set of accounts and understood the 'business' aspect, despite not having been in employment since the birth of my children some 16 years earlier.

I really enjoy being involved in setting the strategic direction of an organization and playing an influential part in decision making.

I have been prepared to contribute considerable time to my roles, so one of the key contributions I have specifically made has been taking the opportunity to 'network' wherever I can, in order to help build on connections between different organizations within the rural and voluntary sectors and beyond. Often this has involved attending conferences and other networking events that paid staff do not have the time to attend. I can represent and provide a presence for the organization at certain key events.

As a trustee of several different organizations which all have some crossover in relevance to each other, I have been able to bring an informed and broader perspective to each of the Trustee Boards on which I sit.

The amount of time I devote to each charity has reduced substantially in the past year due to every organization cutting its governance costs by reducing board meetings to be held quarterly. Finance committees have been absorbed back into the main board business; possibly because income streams have reduced considerably.

On average, I spend six or more days a year on a board's business:

* 4 board meetings – half a day plus travel
* 2 trustee/staff away-days (whole days including travel)
* 2 hours pre-meetings to study board papers
* A 24-hour annual conference plus travel (2 hours each way)
* In addition there is regular email correspondence and e-newsletters to be read (often weekly/monthly bulletins) and external events to attend from time to time.

Sometimes there may be extra-curricular work, for example in a 'task and finish' group to agree a job description and person specification for a new chief executive; sitting on an interview panel to recruit new members of staff.

Trustee boards work best when the CEO regards board members as critical but supportive friends of the organization with whom to share concerns and problems and to work together to find suitable solutions. This does not always happen and board decisions are only as good as the information provided to them by the executive. An experienced trustee can often tease out what the board is not being told by asking the right questions.

It is important that there is mutual respect between the board and the executive. The board, through the chair, needs to ensure good governance procedures are followed and that the board is regularly refreshed. The board needs to take a good honest look at itself from time to time to ensure it is a body deserving of the respect of its executive. I am fortunate that all the boards on which I sit have good relationships with their CEOs but this has not always been the case.

Focus points

It is essential that you get the structure of the executive and the board of trustees right from the outset and that you appoint suitable people to perform for key roles in both.

Hard though it is to avoid, the founder should not be a one-man band, and s/he should be prepared to rely on the skills/experience of others to take up the mantle for the development and smooth running of the organization.

The workload of the executive/staff can be eased by the use of volunteers.

A board of trustees which brings specific and useful expertise to the governance of the organization is the invaluable heart of an organization.

The relationship between the board of trustees and the executive (senior management team), especially between the chair and the chief executive, is crucial to the consistent and effective running of the charity.

Next step

The final foundation block of setting up and running a charity before you get on to the exciting world of fundraising and marketing is the importance of developing a budget, which we'll look at in the next chapter.

5

Developing a budget

What you will learn in this chapter:

- ▶ *The benefits of budgeting*
- ▶ *Identifying new income sources*
- ▶ *How to look at diversifying income sources*
- ▶ *What is the purpose of having a charity reserve?*
- ▶ *The importance of cash flow*

There is just one last part of the administrative jigsaw that needs to be put in place before we move on to the no doubt eagerly anticipated chapters on fundraising and marketing your charity – the bit everyone really wants to start with.

Although I am sure you would prefer to concentrate on the daily demands of running a charity and the direct needs of your beneficiaries, the truth is that the chances of attaining your goal of helping people/your cause will be greatly improved if you plan strategically, and that includes developing a budget. Somehow you have to balance the day-to-day running of the charity with planning ahead. By the same token, when developing a budget, you are trying to balance the visions of the charity with the reality of having to secure the necessary funds to pay for them.

And the golden rule of budgeting is that, no matter how laudable your plans for what you want to achieve or how pressing the cause, you should never try to operate beyond the charity's means. You can only achieve what can be paid for, so the budget needs to be realistic.

Basically, a budget should help you to use your resources to implement strategic plans. It is also a way to set goals for various departments or individuals, and to numerically evaluate performance and accomplishments. Whether it is a budget for the whole organization or a business case for a specific project, it should be carefully planned.

Why set a budget?

Developing a budget is crucial because it can force the management to set priorities depending on how much money the charity has, how much it plans to make and how much it needs to spend. If the executive and the trustee board regularly check how much is spent against how much it was planned to spend, any significant over- or under-spending will be flagged up and then action can be taken, if necessary.

Using a budget helps you to translate abstract goals into measurable objectives – it essentially helps you to measure how the organization's financial performance meets its ambitions. A budget consists of expenditure and income projections. Both are essential but cash flow is king. If all of your expenditure comes in one part of the year and income comes in another, the budget cannot work. Having cash to cover your expenditure is crucial – you will get nowhere running on empty.

One of the side effects of preparing budgets that shouldn't be underestimated is that preparing a budget encourages operational staff to co-operate and co-ordinate with the financial departments who collate the information. Depending on the size and structure of your organization, senior operational and administrative staff should seek input from the people with whom they work and so it works throughout the management structure, and the further it reaches, the more it engenders a sense of ownership and involvement in the staff.

Finally, the main reason for setting a budget is that, if it is well planned and implemented, a budget will ensure that the charity delivery is sustainable and thus it makes its future secure.

Despite the distinct benefits of setting a budget, you should be sensitive to the fact that those not involved in the process – usually the operational or programme staff – can feel differently about budgets. The feedback I hear most commonly is that they feel a budget does not reflect their needs or the frontline reality, and that it stifles creativity and does not take the quality of service in to account due to its emphasis on cost control, especially if it relies on historical information rather than what's happening at the moment. Getting involvement and input from the operational staff and feedback when circumstances change is the only way to make a budget more effective and to keep morale high.

STAYING CREDIBLE

Grant makers and philanthropists know the market and the economic climate as well as you do, and they are aware of what can be achieved. If you approach them and other potential financial supporters with an over-ambitious budget, they will at best be perplexed, and at worst consider your organization amateurish. The easy mistake to make is finding that your support costs (overheads) are too high for your delivery costs. The charity is set up to deliver services, not to support a grand management structure.

In the early stages of your charity's existence, and certainly until you have a proven track record, competing for operational funding will be tough, but showing inflated income projections in your budgeting will not cut any ice with those dealing out the cash.

Remember this: Who benefits?

Charities differ from businesses because the customer who receives the service is usually not the person who pays for it. So when budgeting, there is not necessarily a direct correlation between the services you deliver and the amount of income you generate. This must be considered when combining the income and expenditure aspects of the budget.

BUDGETING CONSIDERATIONS

There is a very helpful budget review checklist on the National Council for Voluntary Organizations' (NCVO) website that can help you to make sure you are asking all the relevant questions of the organization and gathering all the right information when preparing budgets. Here are a few of the more important considerations:

▶ Goals and objectives

Have you developed objectives for the short-term, i.e. the coming year, and for the long term, say a three- and five-year plan, and how do they differ? When formulating the future budget, it can help to evaluate results from the previous year. For example, did you achieve your objectives? If not, was there a justifiable reason or were the budgets unreasonable in the first place? Could a mid-year financial review and taking appropriate action have changed the outcome?

▶ Scheduling

Have you allowed enough time to gather all the forecasting information needed and to fit in the necessary approval processes? Have you allowed for the lengthy lead time for grant requests and multi-year project funding? In my experience, you need at least six months' preparation time before the date from which the budget applies.

▶ Programme delivery and services

When preparing estimates of income and expenditure for programmes/services, it helps not only to budget for new programmes and services but also to look at existing programmes to see if they can justify themselves. Is the organization reaching enough stakeholders? Is a competing organization offering the same service and could your efforts be combined? Should changes be made to the services you offer and how does the income it generates relate to the true cost of the services? The Holy Grail is 'full cost recovery' which covers all of your frontline and support costs. This often places services beyond the reach of many, so this is where a number of funding sources comes in. Are there alternative funding sources available?

▶ Funding

If you review your current income streams, you can not only assess your level of risk, but you can also make sure that you have spread the sources so that you do not have all your eggs in one basket, so to speak. Make sure you diversify so that, wherever possible, you have a mixture of sources covering gifts from individuals and the private sector, grants, contracts and from the open market. Depending on the services you offer, perhaps a change of tack could be profitable – perhaps you should move the focus from seeking funding for the delivery of activities/services (outputs) to 'outcome funding' which puts the emphasis on the change brought about by the outputs rather than the delivery of the outputs themselves.

▶ Fundraising

It is important to evaluate the activities and results of your fundraising team and to decide which type of campaigns have been effective and therefore deserve investment for next year, and which ones are not producing enough results for the effort invested in them. This is called Return on Investment (ROI). Are you simply hosting fundraising events/activities because you have always done so? Can sponsorship be found for certain activities? Do you have a planned giving programme? Will funding continue at the same level or will it be cut due to the economic downturn? Is the organization up to speed for grant requirements?

► Overheads/Expenses

You are looking at ways to improve efficiency in order to reduce costs. This is a wide-reaching remit and you should look at all areas ranging from staff/volunteers ratio through IT requirements to segregation of fixed and variable costs.

► Supplementary budgets

Apart from the overall budget for the organization, there are countless supplementary budgets that can be prepared for specific projects, cash flow projections, capital additions such as building extensions or buying equipment, investment objectives/ income, and many, many more. These should not be mixed up with the core budget and each should only be approved using an individual business case.

BUDGET APPROVAL

Once you are confident that the projections are reliable, your reserves sensible and your budgets realistic, then it is time to seek final approval and this is usually carried out at a trustee meeting designated for this purpose. Before a budget is submitted, a strategic plan should be agreed and not the other way around. However, don't think that that is an end to it for another year. In the interim, you must have systems in place to monitor the budget and to reforecast and make revisions in exceptional circumstances.

Remember this: Budget finance committee

It does not have to be the finance director and treasurer working in isolation who are responsible for preparing budgets and compiling data. Could a budget finance committee made up of finance staff, trustees and even outside members be useful?

Try it now

Does the timing of your financial year end and budgeting process make sense? At Henshaws, we recently moved our financial year end so that it fits in with the approval of our major contracts. Rigidly sticking to the conventional financial year simply meant recalibrating the budget months after it had been 'approved in principle' – a waste of time for all involved.

Remember this: Outside influences

Outside funders sometimes wield enormous influence on the budget as they try to ensure the programmes you offer accomplish their own goals. Always deliver what is best for your charity and do not chase the money. Any fool can get funding for something you don't do.

Reserves

In healthy economic times, it is considered good practice for a charity to hold in reserves perhaps 25 per cent of its annual turnover or funding to cover six months of operations, in order to cover unexpected eventualities and the cost of winding up the organization if funding should cease.

However, in a harsher climate, the jury is still out on just how much a charity should hold in reserves. Too much and it is not best use of donors' money; too little and it is a risk.

In the past, many larger charities have kept too much in reserve. The Charity Commission expects funds donated for a service to go to that service – not sit in a bank.

Under charity law, all charities must spend any income received within a reasonable period, which means you cannot hold money in reserves indefinitely. However, a reserve is the one part of your charity's funds that you are free to spend however you see fit, i.e. it was not donated for a specific purpose.

RESERVES POLICY

A reserves policy makes clear the reasons why you are setting aside money for a reserve rather than spending it on your charity's aims.

The policy is usually drawn up between the executive and the trustee board, and it has to be set out in the trustees' annual report (if the charity has no reserves policy, this too must be stated in the report), so funders, donors and stakeholders can all see that you are using funds prudently. The report should state how much the charity holds in reserve, why it is felt necessary to reserve this amount and what your charity reserves may be spent on.

Obviously, all these considerations need to be taken into account when compiling your reserves policy. Factors to consider when deciding how much to reserve might include the charity's financial circumstances, potential drops in income, a difficult economic climate and unexpected demands for development work. As a rule of thumb, do not use reserves to prop up operational expenditure.

If you decide to set aside money for a specific purpose, for example building refurbishment, then in this instance, it should be made clear that this is separate from the charity's general reserves.

Clearly, it is important to monitor the level of reserves and to review the policy regularly to make sure it is keeping abreast of the charity's changing needs. How you invest the money set aside for the reserves is also another important consideration.

INVESTMENTS POLICY

Once you have decided how much money you wish to set aside as a reserve, you must then decide what to do with those funds. Most charities take external investment advice from experts in the field, which is to be recommended.

All I will say on the subject is that you need to exercise care to spread the level of risk when making investment decisions and that any policy you set should be reviewed regularly. And the other factor worth considering internally, if you plan to follow external investment advice, is whether the choice of investment is in keeping with the ethos of the charity and whether or not you want an ethical investment element.

Develop an investment policy and if possible form an investment committee from executives and non-executives.

Remember this: Budget balancing

There are exceptions to the usual budgeting rule that income and expenditure should match. Sometimes, you make an active decision to use income from investments, i.e. the charity's reserve, to finance initiatives that could not be funded elsewhere.

Case study: Lynette Lace, Finance Director at Brook Advisory Service

All you need to start your own registered charity financially is £5,000 in the bank (according to the Charity Commission) but what you really need to start up is a solid financial plan – how else will you make your charity robust and enduring?

You will no doubt write a plan of what you intend to do with your charity and probably have thought about how you intend to pay for things – but it needs to be a bit more than that to give you (and your funders) the confidence that this is going to work out right. You need to plan your money as well as what you intend to deliver.

There are two main tools needed to help you plan the finances for your charity:
* Budgets
* Cash flows
Neither of these is difficult to construct but without them you have no real money plan and that means an uncertain future.

Budgets

A budget is described as a plan for the future and is normally written for the first year at least (sometimes the first three years). It is also a safety net for future events – allowing us to see in advance where a problem might arise and so plan for that event. It is also a measure of performance – a case of 'this is what we planned to do and this is what we actually did'.

So how do we start? The first thing to do is list all of the income that you are expecting – be realistic at first, think about what you have already secured. For instance don't at this stage include an event say where you think you might raise £5k when actually you have no experience of such events and actually have no real idea how much it might be – although hopefully it will raise more than you planned!

Just start off very basic – this is what we know we have coming in.

Then list all that you have got to pay out – rent, salaries, venue costs, materials, travelling, insurance, etc. Think long and hard as suddenly coming up against a cost that you have to pay when you haven't planned it can end your charity before you really get going. Will you need to pay any professional fees? Bank charges? Buy any equipment? And so on.

Once you have this detail then you can compare one against the other. Does the income you know you have raised cover the costs? If not can you cut costs? Can you share costs with someone else? Can you get volunteers or donated goods?

If you can't reduce costs can you increase income? Fundraising events? Bid for funding from other sources?

These are the questions you need to factor in until the income and expenditure match or (better still) the income exceeds the expenditure.

This means your charity has its first financial plan. It doesn't have to be technical, just try and make it as complete a picture as possible – however that's not quite the whole story.

The thing that often catches people out is cash flow – charities go bust because they can't pay their bills.

So although we can now show your charity has a surplus of income over expenditure, can it pay its bills as they fall due?

What we now need to do is spread the budget that we have just constructed over the months (or even weeks) of the year and place into each month or week the funds that we are expecting in. If you have received funding then check with your funder if they pay all up front (unusual), or at the end of each month, or quarterly in advance or only allow you to claim back funds that you have already spent and so on.

Factor this income into your cash flow – put it into the month/week when you actually have the cash in your hand (or in your bank!).

Now do the same with expenditure – include it in the cash flow when you will actually have to pay it. For instance invoices may be due a month after you have bought the goods, rent may be payable a quarter in advance, salaries are due on the 28th (say) and the PAYE is then due on the 19th. All of these things need to be factored in.

Are there any gaps? Are there months or weeks where you will have to pay things out but the funds to do so are not due until the following month/

week? Do you have enough in hand to manage this? Will you be able to plan your fundraising event in time to get those funds into the bank?

No gaps – no problem!

These two tools are simple ways to help you manage your charity's money, see and plan for problems well in advance and so sustain your charity for the exciting years ahead.

Focus points

Preparing a budget is essential to review how the organization is performing financially.

A sensible budget is vital to keep your charity sustainable.

It is not only the financial team that is involved in budget preparation. All departments should understand the part they play in forming and monitoring the budget and should be involved in data provision and feedback on current and expected scenarios.

Historical data can be useful but this must be balanced with projections for the future, taking into account changing climates and other variables.

Keeping a reserve is prudent management of charity funds but it is essential that you get the figure right and that the amount is invested wisely.

Fundraising projections are notoriously difficult to predict. Be neither too optimistic nor too cautious in estimating fundraised income.

Next step

Now all the structures are in place for the efficient running of the charity, we can turn our attention to the important area of funding, income generation and fundraising.

6

Funding and income generation

In this chapter you will learn about:

- ▶ *The differences between funding and fundraising*
- ▶ *How to have a comprehensive strategy for generating funds*
- ▶ *Central government and local government grant awards*
- ▶ *How to use trusts and grants, including the lottery, for funding*
- ▶ *New ways of income generation for charities*

Finding the funds to support the running of your organization is something that preoccupies all those who run a charity from the biggest to the smallest. In fact, there are whole books devoted to the thorny issue of raising enough money to allow you to do the important work that you want to do.

So here, we can only scratch the surface of the dark art of finding funds. I hope to give you ideas about the various ways you can bring in income but, if you want to go into the subject in more depth, there is a wide range of providers who offer one or two day training courses on fundraising and funding and, in general, these courses may cost to attend but the results in the long term should be justifiable. As your charity grows, so you can think about employing specialist staff within the field to concentrate on this important area but until then, it's all hands to the deck. And although I called it a dark art, the truth is that if you follow a logical, well thought through plan (with a healthy dose of creativity), then getting enough funds to deliver your services should be possible.

The UK's voluntary sector income grew considerably in the decade leading up to 2011, with a total annual income of £38.3 billion in 2010/11, although most suspect the growth has now slowed due to the harsh economic realities. The top ten charities raised £1,717 million between them – that's 15 per cent of all fundraised income in the sector; with Cancer Research UK, way ahead of the rest, raising £418m, and the British Heart Foundation and Oxfam generating £227m and £187m respectively in second and third place. The balance is split between the remaining 162,000 charities that are all competing for a slice of the pie, so you can see why getting your funding and fundraising policy right is essential.

You can get income to support your charity from a variety of different sources, and targeting a combination of different funding and fundraising routes is the best option. Different methods, approaches, skills and techniques are required for each different funding source if you are to get the best results and bring in the biggest sums. And these methods have to be reviewed regularly because the best fundraising tools have a shelf-life. Like most things, something catches the public imagination and becomes in vogue – for example, wristbands in the late 1990s and early 2000s were hugely popular and a highly effective way of raising funds and awareness – and then the popularity started to wane. Make sure that, as part of your strategy, you are part of the trend and that you use whatever is popular at the time to make money while it lasts, and then change your policy and move on to the next popular fundraising method.

So, let's look at funding and income generation in this chapter and then we'll move on to fundraising in Chapter 7.

Remember this: Give a reason

It doesn't matter which source you're looking at – funding or fundraising – and which method you're using, you need to clearly show donors/ funders who or what their donations/grants/funding will go towards and the benefits.

Funding

The main sources of funding for the voluntary and community sector are statutory funding such as health commissioning, European funding (although this has declined considerably), Trusts and Grants including lottery funding, and income generation such as charity shops and other commercial activities.

STATUTORY FUNDING

This generally comes from central government and local authorities and is applied for by grant applications to the relevant department, very often compiled by the operational staff themselves as funding is nearly always delivery related and quite specific about what it can and can't be used for.

There are funds set aside by local and central government specifically to help charities to deliver the services that would otherwise have to be provided by the state. Sadly, at a time of budgetary cuts, especially at local government level, there is not as much funding available as in the past and, some would say, not as much as is required.

Nonetheless, if you are providing a necessary service, you may well qualify for statutory funding and you should make grant applications in good time for that assistance. There are usually strict criteria in place and you may need to be able to show that the programme outcomes fit the policy objectives of that grant/department.

Statutory funding does not always come directly from central government – much of the funding is available through a wide range of government agencies, quangos or non-departmental public bodies, such as the Design Council, the Countryside Commission and the Community Development Foundation.

The Office for Civil Society (OCS), based in the Cabinet Office, set up the Social Investment Business (SIB) in 2009 and this is the largest social investor in the UK.

In the case of local authority grants, every council is different. In the past, each department within the local authority had their own budget which they could allocate to charities and community groups but there have been moves to introduce a one-stop 'corporate' application system where only one form is required.

Although the Coalition Government ended the system of central monitoring of targets, thus allowing councils greater say on how funding money is spent locally, the severe cuts in budgets means that most local authority funding has effectively been slashed.

APPLYING FOR FUNDING

It is vital that, before you write and submit your grant application for statutory funding, you do your research. What's available? How have criteria changed? It can be time-consuming but making sure you direct the right bid to the right department increases your chances of reaping a reward. You can find detailed information on the various sources of statutory funding on the website of the Directory of Social Change – www.governmentfunding.org.uk – and you can also subscribe for regular email updates from them.

You will also need to submit details of some of your internal regulation, for example policies and procedures. Trustees may need to sign these documents (operational teams supply through-puts and financial managers supply budgets) so build in a reasonable timescale for preparation.

You may consider your charity to be too small to be in with a chance of winning these central government and local authority grants, but there is no reason why you should not link up with other charities in the field to bid for the big contracts and tenders. An example of where this has worked to good effect is in the field of prisoner rehabilitation. In 2013, a consortium of charities in the North of England formed to bid for prisoner rehabilitation contracts, in response to the news that 70 per cent of probation contracts were to be opened up to private and voluntary sector providers. The Government's 'Transforming Rehabilitation' strategy means that different delivery providers will be granted payment-by-results contracts.

EUROPEAN FUNDING
There is European funding available but in reality, getting and managing European funding can be complicated and time-consuming, with the vast majority of funds going to the poorer regions of the union's member states.

If you have someone with the time and energy available, you could look for support from the Third Sector European Network (which merged with the NCVO at the end of 2011) and the European Social Fund (ESF), especially if your charity works in the area of employment and skills issues. Nonetheless, I suggest you look at funding closer to home as your first priority.

TRUSTS AND GRANTS
There are roughly 7,500 grant-making trusts and foundations in the UK that give around £2 billion in grants to charities (including religious organizations and educational establishments such as universities) each year.

The larger trusts distribute several million pounds annually, but most trusts are much smaller and only give out grants in the region of several hundred or possibly a few thousand pounds, with research showing that 74 per cent of grants made were for £5,000 or less – only 14 per cent exceeded £10,000.

Grant-making trusts are charities themselves, so they have to spend their money in ways that are for the public benefit. Most trusts derive their income from an endowment given by a wealthy individual, family or company (and are often named after the benefactor), and the interest made is given out in grants. Some trusts are set up as the result of mass appeals, such as Comic Relief, Sports Relief and Children in Need.

There is also a relatively new breed of grant-making trusts which act as a broker for donors and collectors of endowment, either in a local area (a community trust) or in a specialist field (an intermediary trust).

About 70 per cent of trusts and foundations give in the health and social welfare fields, and the arts and recreation also do well from trusts, but it is still worth pursuing if your charity does not fall within these categories, as grant-making trusts will sometimes fund the things that other funders and government will not – new ways to tackle problems, disadvantaged and minority groups facing barriers in accessing services and responses to new or newly discovered needs. They are also keen to fund one-off projects or purchases such as soft play equipment for a playgroup, or short- and medium-term initiatives such as a one-year drug-addiction programme that might, once established, attract longer-term funding from elsewhere.

One example is The Andrews Charitable Trust, established in the 1940s by Cecil Jackson-Cole who was the co-founder of Action Aid and Help the Aged, and could be of particular interest for new and fledgling charities as its niche is funding new voluntary organizations.

According to the latest research by Directory of Social Change (DSC), it appears that grant-making trusts and foundations are continuing to give at a stable level despite the difficult economic climate, but hopes that they might be able to plug the gap left by lost statutory funding are overly optimistic.

LOTTERY FUNDING

The Big Lottery Fund is the biggest lottery distributor, giving out half of the money raised by the National Lottery for good causes, which include the arts, charities and voluntary groups, heritage, health, education, the environment and sports. Lottery funders are the organizations that distribute the 'good causes' money to local communities and national projects.

After the Big Lottery Fund, other key lottery funders include the Arts Council (see useful addresses for the various individual countries), the British Film Institute, Sport England, Sport Scotland plus the Sports Council for Wales and the Sports Council for Northern Ireland, and the Heritage Lottery Fund.

If you explore the National Lottery site for good causes – Lottery Funding www.lotteryfunding.org.uk – you will find all the current information on funding programmes.

Many have online application forms and deadlines by which these must be received. The process can take months so plan well ahead and always check whether they need 'match funding' from another source.

GRANT APPLICATIONS

The problem with applying to trusts is that the research is time-consuming and it takes a certain skill to get it right. That is why most of the bigger charities employ someone or use a specialist freelancer who has experience in grant-application writing, but beware of costs: you can spend a lot with no guarantee of success.

If that's not available to you, before you apply, it is worth checking out the useful advice provided by the DSC on the policies and practices of trusts and foundations and recommendations to applicants. In addition, make sure you read the guidelines provided by the individual trusts and make sure you are applying to the right funder for your cause.

Research is key. There are plenty of websites that can help with finding funding available through search engines. Look at the funding criteria and make sure you meet them. When researching the right trust or foundation for your needs, there are searchable online databases now, including the Directory of Social Change (www.dsc.org.uk).

Meanwhile the major trusts have their own websites and you can find these at the Association of Charitable Foundations or

Charities Direct websites. And to find local trusts, contact your nearest Community and Voluntary Service (CVS).

There are also subscription services such as those provided by Trusts and Foundations (www.trustfunding.org.uk), the Voluntary and Community Sector (www.fundinginformation.org.uk) and Grantfinder (www.grantfinder.co.uk), but make sure you compare fees and check out what you get for your money before paying any fees.

A useful tool for those applying for grants is the Fit4Funding newsletter which updates you on changes in trusts' and foundations' guidelines and any short-term funding offers. You can sign up for a free trial to see if it is of value to you before committing.

Try it now

When you have completed your grant application, get someone from outside the organization to read it through to make sure your application is clear, concise and jargon-free and that it makes sense to a non-specialist.

IMPACT MEASUREMENT

The people responsible for funding and commissioning the services that charities deliver increasingly want evidence that a charity can deliver what it promises as well as lasting change.

According to the New Philanthropy Capital's report, 'Making an Impact', three-quarters of charities report that they measure the impact of their work and 74 per cent of these have invested more in measuring results in the last five years. Moreover, the report suggests that keeping funders happy is the main reason for such efforts. Over half say they have increased their measurement efforts in order to meet funder requirements, while only 5 per cent state service improvement as their main motivation.

INCOME GENERATION

This has been a relatively new development that has grown in the last few decades. No longer do charities rely solely on applying for statutory funding alongside their fundraising efforts; they are now looking towards increased income generation, which ranges from taking on contracts in delivery services in areas such as the community services, health, welfare, education and leisure activities right through to more 'entrepreneurial' ways to generate income such as selling products made by their beneficiaries and selling books/magazines, training, consultancy and other in-house expertise.

Similarly, by applying a little entrepreneurial-thinking to the situation, you might think about providing a service under contract with another agency, perhaps a local or health authority, which is a more cost-effective solution for them. Charity shops have taken on a whole new dimension as they start to sell unrelated items and charity Christmas cards, etc. Some charities are even investigating charging service users or requesting a contribution. If a bricks and mortar charity shop is too ambitious, some charities are now selling items through organizations such as eBay, which has a dedicated subsidiary, known as www.missionfish.org.uk, that raises millions for charity partners.

Of course, if you want to undertake this kind of social enterprise, you may need to set up a separate branch of the charity as a community interest company (CIC) or charitable incorporated organization (CIO), as discussed in Chapter 2. Many charities find that there are distinct advantages to having an independent revenue stream, but beware of tax and VAT levels. Do your research.

Naturally, there are difficulties involved in having an income-generation aspect to your funding plans, not least the risk of the venture failing or losing money. If you want to start small, you can sell Christmas cards, for example, without going to the length of setting up a separate charity, as this is deemed selling for non-primary purpose and, as the risk is low, it is allowed.

Whatever the level of trading, it would be wise to seek advice before going down this route, but luckily there are quite a lot of organizations offering support and advice in these areas. Look to your Local Council for Voluntary Service and Rural Community Council. In addition, you may well have a social enterprise development agency in your area, so check out the Technical Support for Social Enterprise page of the NCVO's

Sustainable Funding Project. If you want to start a charity shop, you're best advised to check out the Association of Charity Shops for fuller details.

Remember this: Sea change

If you bid for delivery service contracts, it means that what, in the past, might have been a funder/funded relationship now becomes a purchaser/provider partnership.

Remember this: Charity shops' gift aid

In 2013, HMRC simplified gift aid claiming for charity shops. Now those who donate items to charity shops can make one-off gift aid declarations, so the charity no longer needs to write to donors once the items have been sold. If you run your shop via a trading subsidiary, you can accept one declaration for the sale of items costing up to £1,000 per annum. If you don't run your shop that way, you can instead receive the same for goods to the value of £100 from an individual donor.

Case study: The Museum of Somerset and The Art Fund

The Art Fund gave a main grant and assisted in a public appeal, with a fund matching grant.

Beyond its main grant giving role, the Art Fund – along with its nationwide network of volunteers – enjoys and has a great deal of experience of working with museums and galleries on their individual fundraising campaigns. Back in April 2010, in a story which captured the public imagination, metal-detectorist Dave Crisp unearthed a hoard of more than 52,000 Roman coins held in a large pottery vessel, in a field near Frome, Somerset. The find – the second largest Britain has ever seen, and, significantly, the largest to have been discovered in a single container – was swiftly brought to the attention of Somerset Museums Service, which determined to secure the whole hoard for the county. It was hoped that the coins, an unprecedentedly large number of which depicted Carausius, emperor in Britain during the third century, would be displayed and researched at the newly refurbished Museum of Somerset in Taunton Castle.

The museum, having approached the Art Fund for a grant to support its planned acquisition, was also keen to make the most of the enormous public interest surrounding the hoard's discovery, and sought our help to do so. At an early display of the coins at Frome Library over 2,000 people including two school groups had queued to see them, giving real hope that a public fundraising campaign would be successful, both in terms of securing money towards a purchase, but also in increasing local interest in the acquisition. Following consideration by the board of trustees, which saw an initial £40,000 grant pledged to the museum's cause, it was decided that the best way to further assist with fundraising would be for the Art Fund to encourage donations elsewhere by offering to match any public contribution up to a maximum £10,000. With this strategy in place our volunteers, hand-in-hand with staff and supporters at the museum, set about organizing events to promote the campaign.

Those involved worked tirelessly to save the hoard, and the success they achieved surpassed all expectations: £13,657 was donated by the public, releasing the full £10,000 of match funding from the Art Fund. Along with contributions from the Headley Trust, the National Heritage Memorial Fund, the V&A Purchase Grant Fund and the Somerset Archaeological and Natural History Society, as well as many smaller gifts, this was enough to retain the Frome Hoard in its proper place.

The hoard went on display for the first time with the opening of the refurbished Museum of Somerset in September 2011 and has since then proved to be a particular draw for visitors. With time now to reflect on the campaign that secured the hoard, Steve Minnitt, Head of Museums in Somerset, is very satisfied. While the initial unearthing of the find and subsequent collaboration between finder, landowner, archaeologists and museum curators have gone down as classic examples of archaeological good practice, Steve has also been glad to witness the forging of far closer links between members of the Somerset Art Fund and the staff of the Museum of Somerset.

The Art Fund (www.artfund.org)

Focus points

The best approach for raising the necessary income to fund services and keep your charity going is to have a good platform comprising of a mix of funding, income generation and fundraising activity.

Central government and local authorities have funds set aside for charities.

Writing grant applications is a specialized skill but training is available, if you can't afford a bid writer.

There are numerous grant-making trusts and foundations, including the Lottery, that give to charities, often for specific projects. Thorough research is required to find what's available and what are the requirements before application.

It can be worth considering the more entrepreneurial approach of income generation to complement your funding and fundraising efforts.

Next step

Let's now turn our attention to the third prong of your money-generating activities – fundraising.

7

Fundraising

In this chapter you will learn:

▶ *How to develop donors and relationships*
▶ *Fundraising routes and committees*
▶ *How to encourage giving via legacies and in-memoriam*
▶ *The importance of the internet for modern charity fundraising*

We have just explored statutory funding and income generation as possible streams of funding but the remaining strand of your finance-boosting efforts should be directed towards raising money from the general public and corporate supporters, i.e. fundraising. In fact, this is a major source of monies, with 24 per cent of total income coming from donations (made by individuals and businesses) and legacies, according to data from the NCVO. The results also show that income from individuals remains the sector's largest source of income, with 55 per cent of the adult population donating to charity in 2011/12 – that's an estimated 28.3 million people who put their hands in their pockets to support a charity. Lots of charities make this look easy but, believe me, it is a lot of hard work and needs a clear plan.

Corporate fundraising

In the great scheme of things, company giving only makes up a relatively small percentage of voluntary sector income – around 3–4 per cent compared with about 35 per cent from the general public. However, if you establish a relationship with a local business, it can reap long-term rewards.

In the past, corporate involvement with charities was largely limited to writing no-strings-attached cheques to a favourite charity on the odd occasion. Yet, the corporate climate is changing. With an increased emphasis on Corporate Social Responsibility (CSR), which means recognizing that a company's operations have an impact on the community at large, more and more companies are becoming involved with charities, voluntary and community groups. Now, the majority of big companies have CSR policies as a way of demonstrating their integrity to their customers while also helping a chosen charity.

As a result of CSR activities and closer relationships with a charity, companies are reporting a boost to staff morale and better standing within the community. In practice, these activities can include staff involvement in fundraising activities for the charity; expertise and skills being made available on a pro bono basis; employees acting as volunteers; donation of products, materials and/or equipment; and the launch of joint promotions, where the company might make a donation in return for every product sold.

In purely financial terms, a company that becomes a supporter of your charity might well be prepared to fund match whatever funds are raised by certain appeals, or to make you its nominated charity for payroll giving schemes or perhaps sponsorship of fundraising events.

A marvellous example of a company that has embraced the CSR ethos is American firm, Salesforce. Its CSR policy is to give 1 per cent of its profit (in the form of products), 1 per cent of its employees' time, and 1 per cent of its equity to charities and other non-profit organizations. Salesforce employees are allowed to do six days of charity work each year and are actively encouraged to support charities of their own volition. This has reaped rewards when it comes to employee motivation and retention.

If you are lucky enough to have a 'special' relationship with a corporate supporter, you must nurture that relationship and invest in it. Make sure that it is not all a one-way street with them giving and you taking … keep them informed, mention them in your newsletters, etc., and keep the staff as well as the management involved at as many levels as possible.

Try it now

Most companies publish their CSR policies. Once again, research is key.

Try it now

Some large companies and media such as radio shows and newspapers have a charity of the year which they and their readers/listeners support in their fundraising efforts. Why not identify a list of such corporate sponsors and approach them to see if your charity could be nominated in a forthcoming year.

Remember this: Make it personal

A study found that donations to company charity campaigns doubled when a photograph of one of the business's donors was included in fundraising efforts.

Raising money from individuals

There are many ways to raise money from individuals, whether that means the man on the street or the top-end, high-network philanthropist and charity supporter, often known in the trade as high value donors. Accordingly, most charities, irrespective of size, capacity or location, have a dedicated team, drawn from staff, volunteers and/or trustees, who are devoted to such fundraising efforts.

This is a sensible approach because there are numerous ways to fundraise from individuals ranging from small- to large-scale events and campaigns, and all need careful thought and planning.

Whether you look at sponsored cycle rides, bag-packing in supermarkets, tin rattling on street corners, a Christmas carol concert or lavish gala dinner, the principle is the same. The question you always have to ask is will the activity return more than the charity has invested in it (Return on Investment). So, if you are community fundraising, for example packing shopping, are you using volunteers? If not, have you factored in the cost of the time of the staff who are packing and, when subtracted from the profit, how much did you make? Basically, was it worth it?

It is the big events with high set-up costs such as a charity dinner dance with entertainment where you have to be especially careful. Fine if those luxury raffle and auction prizes are donated and if the entertainer is giving his/her time freely, but if you have to pay for those things, it's a different story. You might think 'Great' if you manage to raise £8,000 from ticket sales and the raffle and auction, but it's not so good if the whole event cost you £7,500 to set up. What about staff time? This may sound harsh, but not only is it prudent business sense to assess your fundraising in this way, it is also something that can get you into hot water with the Charity Commission if you don't; they require you to spend most of your donated money on your beneficiaries, which is a charitable purpose, while fundraising per se is not a charitable purpose. As a general rule of thumb, you should aim to make sure that the price of a fundraising event or activity should cost no more than a third of the expected income.

However, there is a caveat to putting the emphasis on figures and columns, and that is to say that fundraising is about much, much more than simply generating income. The money that someone raises from running a marathon or attending a dinner is great. However, in real terms, the biggest benefit of fundraising events is that they offer an opportunity to cultivate good and lasting relationships with donors, which could turn them into long-term supporters.

NURTURING DONOR RELATIONS

A database of names gathered from fundraising activities is worth nothing if you don't use it well to foster good relations with your donors and supporters and to keep in touch with them. A welcoming letter or email when they sign up or express an interest, a regular but not too frequent newsletter and the occasional request for support – all these things are important, but a personal thank you letter if and when they donate/raise funds, etc., is essential. This helps to let donors know that their support is appreciated, that you see them as individual people rather than names on a list, and in turn, this helps to foster their relationship with you and encourage their support of your cause.

HIGH VALUE DONORS (HVDS)

All donors should be valued but there are some who will develop a special relationship with the charity and become true supporters, both in terms of investing time and money in your venture. While making sure you do not neglect those on your mailing lists who give once or twice, it is the people who set up a standing order, who give a substantial gift (major donor) or who are prepared to leave your charity a legacy (see below) that need to be nurtured the most.

Moreover, their friends and connections may well be inspired by their passion for your cause – and they may well be prepared to make an introduction for you, if approached sensitively.

The difference between the way you handle your relationship with your donors and with your high value donors (often classed as those who donate more than £1,000 in a single gift) is that you have to have a personal relationship with your HVDs. They may well be prepared to donate again and potentially to give even bigger amounts but you have to make 'the ask' in person and at the appropriate time. This may sound time-consuming but, in reality, you are only talking about a handful of individuals and it is a worthwhile investment of time as the returns from high value donors can be so high.

The relationship needs to develop at a pace that is comfortable for them, and will almost certainly involve taking them on 'seeing is believing' visits to get close to the need plus attention designed to make them feel wanted and to see the range of opportunities for their involvement. By talking about benefits, not features, a close relationship can be built.

We tend to associate philanthropists with the Victorian era – my own charity, Henshaws, was established thanks to an act of Victorian philanthropy whereby in 1837, Oldham businessman Thomas Henshaw left £20,000 in his will to establish an 'Asylum for the Indigent Blind' in Manchester – 176 years on, we're still going strong and have expanded to the whole of the North of England. Today there are plenty of wealthy men and women who continue this tradition of philanthropy. The name that usually springs to mind in this connection is Sir Richard Branson in the UK and Bill Gates in the US, but they are far from alone. The difference between Victorian and modern day philanthropists is that now they want to give their money away in their lifetime rather than as a legacy, and they are doing it earlier – around 50 years old as opposed to 70 in days gone by.

The wealth of 21st century philanthropists is predominantly self-made at 93 per cent across the United States, according to Peter Hero, founder and principal of the US-based Hero Group, established to meet the needs of foundations, businesses, individuals and families who seek to increase the impact of their charitable giving. This shift differs from 40 years ago when 50 per cent of wealth was inherited and the mindset of giving was different. Hero believes that modern day philanthropists such as those from California's Silicon Valley are more interested in giving money to solutions, not problems. They want to invest in ideas to solve problems, it seems. If this is the way that your charity approaches the issues of your cause, then an approach to a recognized philanthropist could be worthwhile.

Remember this: Take it easy

A poll carried out among the readers of *Third Sector* magazine in May 2013 showed that 86 per cent of respondents thought aggressive fundraising damages public trust in charities. You have been warned.

Legacies and in-memoriam gifts

This is an often neglected source of fundraising because smaller charities assume that it is only the large, well-known charities such as cancer, heart or stroke foundations, and animal charities that will be recognized in people's wills, but this is not necessarily the case.

Currently, gifts donated through wills bring in £2 billion a year to charities, representing 13 per cent of all donations, and that figure could rise if charities were more proactive in asking directly.

Clearly, it is not a priority for new and emerging charities as you have to invest considerable time in managing a legacy campaign, but for an established charity, legacies can make an important contribution to your long-term strategy and the sums involved are considerable. The added bonus is that legacy income is generally non-specific so it can be used for core funding.

Some of the bigger charities produce elegant pamphlets that outline the benefits of legacies and the legalities of will writing, which lays the foundation, but it is no substitute for the most effective way of getting a legacy, which is to ask supporters directly if they will include your charity in their will.

If you don't ask, you don't get seems to be the rule of thumb when it comes to legacies, as the latest research shows: according to a trial report published in May 2013 by Remember A Charity – the Institute of Fundraising's long-term campaign to increase legacy giving to charities, three times as many Britons would leave a gift to charities that they are passionate about in their will, if their solicitor reminded them to consider this opportunity. It will be worth keeping local solicitors updated on what you are doing too.

Another area where charities are missing a trick is in-memoriam giving. This is when friends and relatives on the death of a loved one give a financial gift to benefit one of the charities that the deceased held dear, as a lasting memorial. It is a very personal act.

Nowadays, many families ask funeral attendees to leave a gift to charity rather than send flowers and there are other innovations in the way we commemorate death – JustGiving estimates it will have 30,000 in-memoriam pages on its site by 2021. And recent research by Bluefrog shows that most in-memoriam donors would have been happy to give more, if they had been asked. However, a word of warning – if you get the tone of your post-gift communications wrong, you could alienate the donor completely. In-memoriam giving is hugely important to the donor during the bereavement period and a charity can help to give the bereaved a positive memory. With sensitive handling, this can be an opportunity to forge a strong relationship with new donors.

Campaigns

As you've already seen, there are so many different ways to fundraise from coffee mornings to a sponsored parachute jump, and the only limitation is your imagination, as long as you have the staff or volunteers able to devote the time to such activities.

There is however one way to raise substantial amounts and to potentially give your charity a higher public profile that we haven't yet touched upon, and that is to launch a specific appeal or campaign. In 2011, at my charity, Henshaws, we launched an appeal headed by a blind three-year-old called Oscar

O'Sullivan-Hughes to help save a vital patient liaison service at the Manchester Royal Eye Hospital, which helps people live independent lives. The appeal caught the imagination and attention of local press and then the national press, with Oscar appearing on *The One Show*, among others, to publicize the cause. The year-long effort included a variety of events, including two charity fundraising dinners in Manchester hosted by Coronation Street's Paula Lane, who became involved with the appeal after meeting Oscar. Other fundraisers included coffee mornings, beauty treatment offers, cycle rides, a Santa dash, and a zip wire challenge across Salford Quays. There were runners at the London and Greater Manchester Marathon also raising money for the Appeal. Within a year, with the support of the local newspaper, all this concerted effort managed to raise £50,000 which allowed us to secure our commitment to continuing a service at the Manchester Royal Eye Hospital for people with a visual impairment.

Try it now

Make sure that all new contacts who offered you their details – they may have given a gift, or asked to be added to future mailings – receive an introductory welcome communication before their name is added to the general mailing list. There is nothing worse than making a tentative approach to a charity only to receive a generic direct mail appeal for donations as the first piece of communication you receive.

Remember this: Specialist team

It takes special qualities to handle 'supporter relations' sympathetically and effectively but it also takes specialist knowledge to get the most out of fundraising database software, such as Razor's Edge or Donorflex, which are off-the-shelf specialist databases. If you want to use it for more than just printing labels, i.e. for segmentation so you can target the right groups with different mailings and for giving and campaign analysis, then you should consider investing in outside help to set up your database and to train staff in database management. Go to the Institute of Fundraising to find a consultant.

Remember this: Ultimate goal

It is great to raise some decent money from fundraising events such as gala dinners and carol concerts, etc., but never lose sight of the fact that the most important role of such events is the opportunity they provide to follow up and convert certain attendees into long-term supporters and donors.

Try it now

All staff, even those who are not directly involved in fundraising, should be aware of the need to raise funds. Try to keep it on everyone's agenda. So, for example, if a committee is proposing action items, encourage them to also look at ways that they might be able to generate income to offset some of the expenses involved in that action.

Remember this: The long game

Just because you have had one really successful event that raised a lot of money, don't expect them all to enjoy the same results. Fundraising is a long-term game.

Getting Britain Giving

In 2000, the Government introduced a package of measures to simplify and encourage giving to charity through tax reform, including changes to gift aid, payroll giving and donation of shares and securities. The intention was to encourage a culture of planned regular and tax-effective giving. These areas are worth investigating and exploiting as ways of getting additional funds from individuals without you or them having to do anything.

▶ Tax-effective giving

Payroll giving means that donations are deducted from a donor's salary before tax, so each £1 given only costs the donor 80p, if s/he is on the standard rate tax band, and it costs 60p if you are a higher rate tax payer. The plan allows employees to support any charity they choose with this regular monthly donation. The scheme is administered by an approved payroll giving agent but the only way it can really be worthwhile is if a corporate supporter encourages all employees to sign up for the scheme.

Details about such tax-effective giving initiatives can be found on the website of the Institute of Fundraising.

▶ Gift aid

Gift aid is the most widely used and recognized of the tax-effective giving mechanisms and any charity that ignores this opportunity to get money back from the Government is missing a trick. The principle of gift aid is that HMRC will return to a registered charity the basic rate tax that donors have already paid on any contributions they give you.

If you have the man-power and/or resources, by making sure donors are provided with a gift aid declaration for every donation, and chasing up by phone or in writing all donors who give without making a declaration to ask if they would kindly do so, you could raise the percentage of your gift aid donations to circa 50 per cent, which seems to be about the best you can hope for.

However, the Government is trying to make the system easier. From April 2013, the Gift Aid Small Donations Scheme (GASDS) allows charities to claim a payment equivalent to gift aid on cash donations of £20 or less (with an overall limit per charity) without the need for the donor to complete the declaration paperwork, or the requirement for the donor to be a tax payer. This should allow most charities to claim up to an additional £1,250 from HMRC for very little extra work – and it might encourage the ratio of gift aid donations to rise.

The other development in this field is that the gift aid filing system is now available online. Charities Online (www.hmrc. gov.uk/charitiesonline) allows you to make repayment claims electronically, and the paper filing system was phased out in September 2013.

You need to keep good records for gift aid as HMRC often makes surprise audit visits to small charities to check that the gift aid system is not being abused.

Try it now

If you operate a gift aid policy, it is worth contacting your supporters (who might be higher rate tax payers) to let them know that they can reclaim the difference from HMRC between the basic rate of tax on which gift aid is based and the higher rate that they have actually paid.

The internet and social media

Although technically this is just one of the many methods of fundraising from individuals, it represents such an exciting new opportunity for charities that I have devoted a whole section to the subject.

Admittedly, it was originally the preserve of the younger generation, but as everyone gets more used to moving cash online and as social media is now an integral part of the lives of increasing numbers of older people, so you ignore it as a means of reaching your supporters at your peril, as the power of collecting lots of impulse micro-donations from social media and the internet is proven.

At the very least you should set up a website and perhaps some social media using great video clips, photos and interesting bits of news to establish a compelling, attractive and interesting online presence. Using multimedia formats in your online content to illustrate your message will not only attract new donors but it will help to retain the interest of existing supporters and service users.

You are also more likely to gain fans if you limit self-promotion to about 5 per cent of what you say, according to technology guru, Guy Kawasaki. He recommends that you devote the other 95 per cent to great content on interesting topics related to your cause. Much of that can be links to other people's articles, videos and photos, etc., that position your area of interest and your cause well.

With so much information being readily available online, it's important to have full transparency if you want to engender trust and loyalty. In fact, a recent survey of donors carried out by ethical investment company Oikocredit showed that 48 per cent are more likely to donate to charities that are transparent about their investments and reserves. A lot of charities are moving to publishing their annual report and accounts online and these can also be accessed via the Charity Commission website.

If you can encourage forums and discussions, and you then comment on what your supporters and followers have to say, you can get people to feel passionate about you and your cause, but remember to stay positive and constructive in these dialogues – don't ever get drawn into pointless arguments with 'trolls' (nay-sayers and hecklers who make a nuisance of themselves on purpose).

And it is not just Facebook, there are other social media platforms that are growing in popularity such as Twitter, Pinterest, Tumblr and Instagram and you can use these too in order to forge relationships with a new audience so that they then share your message with their own networks.

Finally, research shows that on average smartphone users check their devices around 150 times a day, so it is essential that your charity is mobile friendly. Make it as easy as possible for supporters to find, interact and donate to you via their smartphone.

All this may come naturally to some individuals in the team but it is a specialist area, especially setting up websites and organizing the sending out of e-newsletters, etc., so once again, you may want to invest in some specialist training or even outsourcing it altogether. In early 2013, Google launched a free initiative designed to help 30,000 small- or medium-sized charities to boost their fundraising by improving their digital skills. Google even gives grants to charities to help improve their web presence. Look out for initiatives such as these.

CROWD-FUNDING

Crowd-funding, as a way of raising money for charities and social enterprises, has become higher profile and more popular since the internet has made it easier to connect funders with those looking for finance. Crowd-funding is the phenomenon where projects, charities, and start-up businesses attract finance through small contributions from many sources. In 2012, the innovation charity Nesta published a report that estimated that crowd-funding could raise £4.7bn a year for UK charities by 2016.

Sites such as Kickstarter for creative projects, Indiegogo for ideas and Peoplefund.it for general causes have all grown in popularity in recent years and represent great potential for small charities. The bigger charities do not want to miss the crowd-funding boat entirely so, in recent years, some have set up their own interpretation of crowd-funding. For example, Leukaemia & Lymphoma Research launched its own challenge-based platform, Pledgeit, in 2012. It offers an opportunity for existing supporters to challenge family and friends to perform a test – it could be anything from a marathon to a bungee jump – and they pledge money in return.

Since this is all fairly new territory for the voluntary sector, it is difficult to know which skills and how much effort is needed in order to be successful. It's early days as yet, but it looks as though crowd-funding could potentially become a mainstream way of raising funds in the future.

Remember this: E-newsletters

Your e-newsletter is not a carbon copy of the paper version – it requires shorter bursts of text and electronic links to your website for a fuller picture of what's going on.

Remember this: Protecting supporters' identity

If you have an electronic following, you have a duty to protect their identity, so make sure names are not shared in the 'cc' box of a newsletter or electronic mailing, for example. You might think that is elementary, but you'd be surprised how many charities make this simple mistake. Clearly, you must abide by the Data Protection Act when dealing with any personal details from donors.

Case study: Patrick Boggon, Director of Tarnside Consulting (www.tarnside.co.uk)

When people set up charities they give dreams the potential to become reality, and make the world a better place. I have worked with charities for 20 years and continue to be enthralled and inspired by people who see a need that should be met, or a wrong that should be put right, and set up a charity to do just that. Setting up the charity, and perhaps drawing a group of people around them with similar ambitions, the possibilities are endless – given the right mix of vision, support and funders – to make the world a better place.

Dreams can be made possible by fundraising, which is essential for nearly all charities and which has been the focus of my work as a consultant. My initial advice for anyone setting up in charitable fundraising would be to bear the following principles in mind:

▶ Get to grips with your ratios

Work out how much it is costing you to raise every £1 that comes in. This figure, usually expressed £x:£1 will show you how efficient your fundraising is. It is important not to spend too much on fundraising, which would be inefficient, but equally important not to underinvest and expect to raise vast sums with no investment. Some figures against which to benchmark your performance: Trust and Foundation fundraising £7 raised for every £1 spent; Corporate Funding £4.43:£1; Memberships £3.54:£1; Major Donors £3.17:£1 and Special Events £1.94:£1. (2010/11 figures, from the annual Fundratios report by the Institute of Fundraising).

▶ Decide where to approach

There are a lot of ways to fundraise, and a lot of markets from which to fundraise. Some will be ideal for your charity, some will be a waste of time and you will need to find the processes and markets to suit you. If you have a large, well-heeled and enthusiastic group of supporters who are naturally inclined towards organizing balls, donating to and bidding at charity auctions, then major events may be for you, although they don't create huge returns. If, alternatively, you are a collectively owned farming co-operative, this may not be for you: there will be other, better ways of engaging with potential donors.

You will also need to consider what sort of funding you need: is it unrestricted (that you can spend on any aspect of your operations, such as paying staff or heating the office) or restricted (funding for a specific appeal such as a new roof)? Some forms of fundraising lend themselves to one or the other. For example, friends groups or regular givers are a good source of unrestricted income, while major gifts from individuals tend to be tied to specific projects.

▶ Hedge your bets

A common pitfall for young charities is a total reliance on one income stream. Many charities contact us when a single source of funding, such as the local council, has stood them in good stead for the first year or two, then has dried up as priorities change and the funding is withdrawn. Healthy charities have a range of income streams which makes them resilient and gives several people or organizations a stake in their success.

In my experience, a charity is likely to succeed in fundraising when it achieves a good return on investment, has a mixture of income sources and gets some large gifts.

People running charities succeed when they are willing to try (and sometimes fail), and when they monitor progress, and change course if things aren't working. Doggedness is a great virtue in fundraising – persisting with something that won't work is less helpful.

So much theory is one thing – but no doubt, you need some practical advice too. If you were to call into Tarnside's office for a bolstering chat, my advice on early fundraising sources would be to head to the library and have a look through the Department for Social Change's Guide to the Major Trusts. There should also be a local one covering your area. Read the user guide and then research charities that might support you. Write them a tailored application, following their guidance.

Go and speak to your local council – if you have a plan which will improve life in their area, they should be able to help. Councils sometimes control local charitable trusts so they may be able to advise on these too.

Think about who's involved already and who should be. Engage with them, ask for their support, and build up a base of supporters who might advocate on your behalf and even fund you.

Take heart and forge ahead: your plans can become a reality and you have the potential to leave the world a better place than you found it. There are multitudes of charitable trusts and philanthropists, large and small, out there – evidence that people do want to change the world, and are willing to support generously those who will.

Focus points

Developing good relations with corporate supporters leads to ongoing fundraising opportunities.

With greater emphasis on CSR policy, corporate fundraising looks set to grow.

There are lots of ways to fundraise and lots of markets to fundraise from.

Take special care of your high value donors, but remember that all donors are people, not names on a list.

Make sure you have a range of income streams.

The internet and social media is an exciting and expanding opportunity for fundraising.

Don't neglect the monies that legacies and in-memoriam donations can bring.

If a fundraising appeal captures the attention of the media and the imagination of the public, it can produce remarkable results.

Always thank your supporters.

Next step

With the charity running effectively and ways to generate income covered, we should now turn our attention to how you market and publicize your charity and your cause.

8

Marketing and publicity

In this chapter you will learn:

▶ *How marketing can help the organization*
▶ *What the real role of marketing should be*
▶ *How marketing fits in with the rest of the organization*
▶ *Which marketing tools might work best for you*

In my experience, charities know how important it is to get the message out there to the general public about the wonderful work that they do. They understand the value of good marketing and publicity and that it can increase support, offer new fundraising opportunities and heighten brand awareness, but not all have the means or the expertise to do it properly. Firstly, there is often not enough money to spend on a marketing budget (and it is one of the first things to come under threat in times of austerity), and secondly, they are aware that donors do not want to see their money being frittered on expensive marketing campaigns, TV commercials or glossy ads.

And the research bears out these fears – in a survey carried out by nfpSynergy, a research consultancy dedicated to the not-for-profit sector, 41 per cent of respondents were concerned about charities spending funds on big marketing campaigns and advertising.

Although you may think that the main role of marketing for a charity of your size is to focus on newsletters, leaflets and websites, in fact, the most important function for a charity of any size is to convey what your charity is all about – its vision, mission and values – and to ensure service users are aware of your services. In order to do that, you need to have a clear 'brand' image that your executive, all the staff and trustees understand and that is simple, clear, motivating and realistic. This is far more important than arguing about typefaces and colours of leaflets. And finally, to achieve this strong brand, you must know your target audience and understand their needs. There's more to marketing than meets the eye, isn't there?

Understanding marketing

As the leader/founder of a modern charity, you need to understand the importance of your charity's image in the eyes of the outside world and whether or not what is seen does justice to the work that you do, your core values and your mission. Your reputation is crucial and needs to be protected and projected, especially in difficult economic times where you have to compete for funds in order to deliver the much-needed services to your beneficiaries.

The impression that you make (however you make it) is especially important for a charity because often donors/ supporters do not personally experience the services/ programmes you deliver, so what else can they judge you on other than reputation and image? Investing in communicating your brand, which encapsulates your reputation, your ideals and your values, so that it does justice to your work is hugely important and it takes more than just designing a nice logo. If they have no direct experience of your work, your reputation and image is what helps people to make up their mind when deciding whether to give financially, whether they are interested in what you have to say and whether they will support you.

Marketing and the rest of the organization

Marketing directors sometimes feel disadvantaged in the board room because they are dealing with intangibles. Telling the executive and trustee board that they should invest scarce resources in marketing because it will raise awareness and generate income is guaranteed to put off some people if there are no hard numbers to back up such a claim.

This is always a problem for those who deal in something that is largely unquantifiable. However, there are plenty of charities that have done the research and the figures support the claim. For example, the charity Teach First, which works to end inequality in education, carried out research in 2011 that showed awareness of its brand had risen among graduates (its target audience) by 40 per cent after its rebrand. As a result, an additional 4 per cent had applied to join Teach First's Leadership Development Programme. It took far longer for SCOPE, formerly The Spastics Society, to establish its new brand.

When trying to measure the Return on Investment (ROI) of marketing, it is harder to gauge the qualitative effect that it is having than the quantitative effect such as income raised or increased attendees. However, just because it is intangible does not mean that it does not have a value. Increasingly, charities are now talking about Social Return on Investment (SROI) which is still an intangible – it can be estimated but never proven. For example, if the alcohol addict you work with stops drinking, is it because of your work with them or because it would have happened anyway? There will be statistics available on the incidence of those who fall off the wagon – if your client group falls outside the average figures, you can use that difference as your SROI. This is currently very trendy but be wary of consultants offering magic results. You can work it out for yourself.

You can also get a handle on the qualitative impact of your marketing and whether or not your goals have been met by getting feedback from the groups you are trying to help and from your target audience.

Remember this: Intangibles

The harder it is to see or measure the benefits, the more your marketing team has to work at encouraging people – staff and supporters – to bring it to life in their own minds.

Remember this: SROI

SROI was developed originally to help charities to show the financial impact of their work, either so they could demonstrate to a funder that their ROI had been achieved, or to support funding bids. However, it can also be used to measure the impact of other intangibles such as marketing results, even though it must not be forgotten that SROI is an intangible itself.

BRAND AND STRATEGY

The marketing team cannot work in isolation. The message about the charity that the marketing team convey to the outside world comes from the top – it is born of your strategy development. When coming up with your strategy development, you should have identified your core values, ambitions and mission – or whatever you care to call it – and it is the job of Marketing to bring those principles to life for the public and for supporters. How your charity is represented must complement your strategic development and everyone involved in those decisions, i.e.

the executive and non-executive boards, must understand the importance of all singing from the same song sheet, so they too can project this vision. Your brand is an expression of who you are, what you stand for and what you do. Clear leadership is needed in this area – all involved can argue for hours about descriptive words, so get a majority behind you and move on.

The other key area where it is important for marketing and strategy to dovetail is when your future strategic plan is moving in a new direction – clearly the person in charge of brand development needs to work closely with those working on strategy, and all the affected departments. In these situations, a special brand steering group could be set up so that everyone knows what is happening at every stage.

BRAND AND DELIVERY

Those responsible for the day-to-day service delivery of your charity are not often privy to the machinations behind how brand image is formed but it is often forgotten that they are the public face of your charity. It's important that they too are aware of the value of your reputation and the importance of raising awareness.

In fact, committed and engaged staff and volunteers are what gives your brand authenticity – in many ways, they bring your brand to life and the services they provide are your greatest brand asset, as it is they who represent your charity, your values and your ambitions to the outside world.

Try it now

Take a look at your strategic business objectives and goals. Do they link with your brand platform, namely the vision and values on which the strategy is founded? Think about a brand you admire and consider why and how it works.

Remember this: Teamwork

It is essential that the marketing and fundraising teams work together in harmony for the charity to succeed.

The tools of marketing

Once you have decided how much you can spend on marketing, choosing the right tools for the job is critical as there are so many different avenues and methods from which to select.

WEBSITE

Every charity, irrespective of size, is now expected to have a website. It can serve many purposes from publicity and communicating the services on offer to boosting fundraising. Its design will be determined by what you want it to do for you and how much you can afford to spend on it.

If you are a large charity, you will perhaps have an IT specialist who will work closely with the marketing team in the design and look of your website. For smaller charities, do not fall into the enticing trap of getting some friend of a friend who 'knows a bit about computers' to design your website. It is a false economy. Since most potential clients/donors will look at your website to draw their conclusions about you, it must look professional and serve the function of projecting your brand image successfully. Instant and often subconscious first impressions of your charity and its personality are all bound up in the logo, layout and content.

You can find a decent web designer who will do the job for you for in the region of £1,000, although of course you can pay more if you go to a larger design agency.

Whether or not you have a web master who hosts your website and posts content for you, or you have the ability to upload content yourself is a decision for you. Either way, it must be easy to update your site regularly, and some of the key elements to include on your website are as follows:

▶ A homepage that introduces your organization – what you do, where you do it and how people can get involved (lengthy bumf on the history, the founder and the current staff can be put elsewhere)

▶ A regular update – possibly a blog

▶ Online donation facilities

▶ Reciprocal links to other organizations and companies that support your efforts.

You can bring the work of your charity alive to web viewers through video, audio, photos and text. Incorporating these multimedia formats into your content to illustrate your impact will help you to attract new donors and retain existing supporters. Forums and chat rooms can also be a way to interact with your followers. But even if you don't go for this option, using Google Analytics, for example, means you can find out a great deal about them anyway – for example, the most popular content on your website, as well as the search terms that brought people to your site in the first place. This gives you a wealth of valuable data about your supporters' online behaviour and potentially their attitudes to your work. Even if the feedback is critical, understanding what is being said about your cause online is useful – and this way, you get a chance to answer their criticisms and address problems before they escalate.

Remember this: Distributing video

YouTube has set up YouTube for Non-Profits to make it easier for charities to make and distribute emotive video of the people, animals or causes that they help. This 21st century way to reach into people's homes and hearts can transform your charity from being just a name and logo to something real and tangible – something to get passionate about. For example, a blind person mountain biking (yes, that's right) could stimulate enough interest for someone to get involved in a charity that helps blind people.

Try it now

It is worth investing a bit of time in comparing the different online donation providers for your website – what they offer and how much. You will need one that provides gift aid collection at source and everything else is optional. Most are quite reasonable but this online giving is an important service – you don't want to scrimp on the provider if it means that you don't get donor information promptly, for example, as a quick gift acknowledgement could mean a donor returns, whereas a poor service or delayed acknowledgement could leave them feeling dissatisfied.

NEWSLETTER

A newsletter is a proactive way of reaching an existing and a new audience, wherever they may be and another opportunity to share news and to reinforce the message about your work and what you stand for.

You can send both printed newsletters and e-newsletters to keep in touch with donors and supporters, but they require a different style. The e-newsletter is punchier and probably more visual, whereas the print version will in all likelihood be lingered over for longer so the prose can be more lengthy.

In an e-newsletter you can put snippets of news and links to your website for more in-depth information. And you should always include a link to the 'Donate Now' page on the website.

However, don't dismiss the value of the traditional print newsletter – it may be the only way to reach some of your older supporters. A print newsletter will be seen not only by the addressee but many others with whom it may be shared. It is present for the duration of the month/quarter on the cover, so it will continue to be shared and circulated throughout that time.

Remember this: Reminders

Always put a calendar of forthcoming events on your newsletter so people can pencil them in to busy schedules well in advance, and always have contact details for the relevant person in case someone wants to raise a query.

Remember this: Beware nuisance marketing

The Information Commissioner's Office has been granted new powers to fine organizations, including charities, up to £500,000 for making unwanted contact with the public through marketing emails and texts. These measures are really aimed at aggressive marketing by companies, especially nuisance live or automated phone calls, but it's still a wise precaution to make sure you meet or exceed good practice when it comes to using texts, emails and phone calls for fundraising and marketing.

SOCIAL MEDIA

Social media can be a cost-effective way for your charity to engage with your supporters and followers and it should be an integrated part of your marketing plan. Although it takes a little time to set up and manage, it is an invaluable tool that allows you to market and publicize the purpose and mission of your charity to a wide community. The same principle applies – control your message.

In the UK, Facebook, Twitter and LinkedIn have the biggest share of the audience. You can link accounts across the three media to save time and effort. So if you 'tweet' on Twitter, it will automatically be posted on your Facebook and LinkedIn accounts.

Obviously, the tone of what you say should reflect what you are all about, and like the website, the content should be alive and buzzing with positive news stories about your charity. If you put social buttons at the bottom of each story, it allows followers to share and discuss with their own networks, offering the possibility of the story becoming viral.

Although social media is undoubtedly a prime tool for marketing, there is a flip side. What if your reputation is being tarnished on social media? Should a negative story break about your charity and its actions, or should someone have unflattering feedback, it is not ideal by any means, but better to know about it than for it to be going on while you remain unaware.

Make sure your marketing team monitors what is being said about your organization online by setting up searches for your name on Twitter and Google Alerts, and regularly reading your Facebook posts. If you spot anything negative that is spreading, act straightaway. Work out your communication response and get your version of events out there immediately. Never ignore it – rather give a clear and calm reason for any actions taken, empathize with any negative effects of these actions and explain the steps you are now taking. Respond as often as you feel is necessary if the debate continues. But don't forget such incidents are rare and social media is overwhelmingly more of a force for good in the charity sector than a disadvantage.

Here are a few more tips that should ensure social media supports your marketing efforts:

▶ You can increase your social media audience by 'hash tagging' the themes, subjects and appeal names so that your posted content will appear in searches for the key words used. For example, #charity, #henshaws, #oscarappeal.

▶ Similarly, by 'tagging' other users within your post, it will then appear on that person's or organization's page as well, and will be visible to their network of connections.

▶ Offer to connect with other charities that have a similar remit and 'retweet' or share some of their content as this will be seen by their contacts too.

▶ Join 'pages' and 'groups' that have a similar mission, and don't be afraid to ask questions or comment on other posts and to seek opinions.

▶ Get your supporters with large followings – celebrities, for example, to retweet your messages.

Remember this: Popularity

Admittedly an inexact science, but how many likes a story receives on Facebook, the number of Twitter followers and Facebook friends, and the levels of activity within these forums can be an indication of popularity and interest that is useful feedback for your organization.

Try it now

Why not empower your staff – or some of your staff – to use social media to promote the qualities of your charity. They can make great ambassadors. If you are anxious that they may damage your image, perhaps that is a sign that you need to revisit your organization's values, key messages and tone of voice, and make sure they are understood and supported by all staff.

THE PRESS AND MEDIA

Nurturing a relationship with the media is an important function of the marketing department. And, if you don't have a marketing person, then it's a job that an appointed person on your team needs to take on.

There are numerous media outlets from free weekly newspapers to regional television and radio stations. All are looking for stories to fill the public's new insatiable appetite for stories 24/7. Through the media, you can reach thousands or even millions of people and it costs only time and effort on your part.

Journalists are looking for a good story. They are especially keen to hear about any human interest story where you have helped someone to triumph against the odds or to make enormous progress. Or perhaps you have a story that has direct relevance to a local readership, i.e. your new initiative will create jobs or boost the local economy. This could be a story about your local corporate supporters. Global and environmental issues are also popular – perhaps your charity is protecting a rare butterfly found on local wasteland.

All of these stories are current and will resonate with readers, viewers and listeners. When you email your news release to the various newsrooms, attach a good high-resolution photo (or low-res version and say hi-res available on request) that features people and is visually interesting (i.e. not two people standing in front of your logo) if you can, as this can help to guarantee inclusion.

If you have good relations with a number of journalists, you can always ring or email them with an idea for a story and ask what sort of angle would be of most interest for them. Getting journalists to visit and see what you do for themselves is always a good move, but remember that these are time-pressed people who are constantly working to deadlines, so they will only come out of their offices for a really good story.

The other way that the media could help your charity is if you seek a celebrity or high profile ambassador. They can ignite passion and enthusiasm in the public better than anything else. It was Bob Geldof back in 1984 who first showed how celebrities can sway the opinion of the ordinary people more effectively than any politician, with Band Aid becoming the fastest selling single ever, and Live Aid being broadcast to 160 countries in the biggest charitable appeal ever known.

That might be a bit ambitious, but the principle holds true. If you can get a high profile or celebrity supporter on board, they will spread the word about your charity to a wider audience and publicize your work on their own social networks.

At Henshaws, we have several celebrity and high profile supporters who all do their bit. TV presenter Mark Edwardson has acted as MC at gala dinners, *Countdown* hostess and *Gadget Show* presenter Rachel Riley supported the Oscar Appeal, and *Coronation Street* actress Paula Lane and her fiancé, Tom Shaw of *The Bill*, ran the London Marathon for us and also went on *Celebrity Mrs & Mrs* and won £30,000 for Henshaws, not to mention raising our profile on a national TV show. The social media went bonkers.

Other charities have used television to raise their profile by getting involved in a relevant storyline in soap operas and TV dramas, films and documentaries. Admittedly, these opportunities have not always been generated by the charity – sometimes the approach has come from the production companies for example, but responding positively to such approaches and making the most of them is a shrewd marketing move. Moreover, there are occasions where you can be proactive. If you know your area of expertise is going to crop up in an upcoming current affairs programme, you can offer your expertise to the producers. You can also use the designated hashtag for the TV programme to join in Twitter conversations and reach new audiences. As the expert in the field, people will retweet your comments. You can also produce live blogs during a relevant broadcast so that the content on your website matches what people might be searching for, inspired by what they are watching on the programme.

Try it now

Practise writing a press release about a recent event or news story. Make sure you include a snappy heading which sums up the essence of the story in one line and that the first paragraph contains all the key points. Subsequent paragraphs can contain succinct quotes and fuller details. There should always be a contact name and phone number and it should be dated. Have a go... it's a skill that takes practice to hone.

Remember this: Press photographs

Before sending photos of children or vulnerable adults to the media with press releases, confirm that you have the necessary permissions for them to be published.

Remember this: Fairs and festivals

If your charity works purely at a community level, local festivals and fairs can be a great opportunity to get out and meet people and to explain what you are doing. Most people are feeling upbeat at these events, so it's easier than usual to engage strangers in conversation and maybe get them switched on to your cause.

Case study: Blue Cross

Blue Cross has an amazing history. Originally founded in 1897 as Our Dumb Friends League, it helped injured animals on the war fields of the Balkan, First and Second World Wars. It also established the world's first animal hospital in London in 1906, which is still operating today.

Despite helping pets for 115 years, the charity has low brand awareness, especially when compared to the Red Cross which is well known for helping people. For many, the blue cross is a symbol that represents a retail sale, like the one that runs at Debenhams. So the charity updated its brand identity for the first time in 60 years.

▶ Laying the strategic foundations

Interviews were carried out with the charity's directors and trustees to establish how they viewed the brand and to assess their appetite for change. A communications audit of current materials was also carried out alongside an audit of other animal welfare charity brands. The audit found that while Blue Cross had a consistent brand identity it was lacking in warmth and personality.

Perceptions-based research with the charity's main audiences was also conducted to inform the future brand direction. The charity had prided itself on championing the relationship between people and their 'companion animals', terminology that it had used for many years. However, the research found that supporters didn't really understand the phrase 'companion animal' and wanted a clearer focus on helping pets. This led to a new vision: 'every pet will enjoy a healthy life in a happy home', and a brand essence of 'healthy happy pets'.

▶ Visual identity: bringing the brand to life creatively

Research explored whether a name change was required to inspire and acquire new supporters. This established that the name was not a barrier to engagement and that knowledge of the charity's heritage helped to build trust. The short and simple strapline 'for pets' was added alongside the name to add greater clarity.

Three concepts for a new visual identity were tested across all the audience segments, with particular attention paid to the views of potential future supporters. The creative options were tested using qualitative focus groups and a quantitative online consumer panel to make sure the new brand would appeal to the right target audience segments.

The new Blue Cross logo is softer and friendlier to reflect the caring nature of the Blue Cross. It has soft rounded edges and is made up of two overlapping hearts, which look a bit like a plaster. The logo shape is used throughout designs as a graphic to ensure the identity is consistent. The main typeface reflects the logo with a soft friendly appearance, supported by a core palette of shades of blue.

There are three styles of photography within the guidelines – pets in need, Blue Cross in action, and healthy happy pets – to allow effective storytelling and fundraising. The focus of the photography is always on the pet with eye contact to heighten the emotional connection and to establish the important 'aahh factor'.

www.bluecross.org.uk

First published in the *Branding Inside Out* Best Practice Guide, available from www.charitycomms.org.uk

Focus points

Make sure your website reflects your charity's personality and showcases your work.

Have an active presence on the major social networks and convey your message through them.

Use video, audio, photos and text content to bring your charity's work to life.

Use Google Alerts to find out what's being said about you.

Heighten your profile so that the print media, radio and television turn to you as the leaders in your field.

Celebrity or high profile supporters can publicize your charity to great effect.

Involve staff, keep them informed – they like to see the charity getting recognition.

Next step

We have looked at how you can help to shape the external response to your charity, now let's look at how internal team dynamics can affect the productivity and effectiveness of your organization.

9

Team dynamics and staff development

In this chapter you will learn:

▶ *About the importance of good leadership*

▶ *How to build your team*

▶ *Ways to get people to understand each other's roles and function*

▶ *The role of volunteers*

▶ *About goal setting and motivation*

▶ *Ways to get your wider community of supporters and beneficiaries more involved*

Many small charities start as the vision of one individual who, through sheer force of character and determination, gets the project off the ground. A few committed early pioneers then come on board to help that individual make his or her dream to make a difference into a reality. As the seeds of the organization take root and the real need becomes apparent, so you build on your original concept and the charity becomes bigger and more complex. As staff come on board, so the founder has to let go of the reins a little and to delegate – s/he simply cannot do it all on their own any longer. Sound familiar?

Wherever you are along that journey, you will face the unique problems that each phase of the charity's growth presents. In this chapter, we will look at some of the obstacles involved in becoming a bigger team, and how to get staff motivated and working well together as a team, so that your organization can reach its full potential.

Leadership

By now, you have probably realized that it is neither practical nor desirable for the founder to continue to be an irreplaceable one-man band. Hopefully, when the organization grows to a mixed team of staff, trustees and volunteers, you will be able to delegate to people with the right skills and experience who are filling the essential roles. Alternatively, you have managed to mould your motley group of founder members into a homogenous team that uses their skills to best effect. Either way, you have a team around you, and you now need to show some leadership qualities as you take the charity forward in order to meet the tricky economic and operation challenges that you may face.

At Sandhurst, they taught me to have a clear plan and communicate it effectively as sooner or later you may not be around to carry it out. The same principle applies here, namely you want the charity to continue if you are not there.

First and foremost, let us recognize the fact that leadership is not the same as management. As a manager, if you are promoted into a leadership role, it is a common mistake to carry on doing what you have always done. Leadership is a different skill. Leaders have the ability to rally employees around a vision and are often willing to take risks in pursuit of the vision. Meanwhile, managers are adept at executing the vision systematically and directing employees on how to do so. By contrast, managers are often risk-adverse.

The principal role of a leader is to make decisions and to take a strategic approach, and you have to be ambitious principally for the cause, the mission, the work – not for yourself. That doesn't necessarily mean you have to be autocratic where you call all the shots. Your leadership style might be democratic, where you prefer consensus and you listen as you lead, or your role might be paternalistic so you have the best interests of your team at heart but whatever your style, as a leader you work to your strengths and take responsibility for your actions and decisions. In his best-selling book, *Good to Great*, Jim Collins states 'Leadership is not about being "soft" or "nice" or purely "inclusive" or "consensus-building". The whole point…. is to make sure the *right decisions* happen – no matter how difficult of painful – for the long-term greatness of the institution and the achievement of its mission, independent of consensus or popularity.' And this leadership needs to be delivered outside the charity as well as internally, so you will be setting the lead for supporters as well.

Some leaders have a gift for turning a charity around, changing the culture or getting a charity to stand on its own, while others are good at leading a charity as it consolidates its place in the community. Recognizing that your strengths are suited to certain circumstances means that you also need to understand when it is time to either change your approach or to move on.

As a leader, one of your greatest responsibilities is to communicate effectively, and sometimes the messages you have to deliver are unpalatable. You must be clear and you must reiterate key messages time and time again, because people may not get it first, second or even third time around. However, do remember to delegate and then let people get on with it.

If you want to explore how to lead in partnership and work collaboratively with other sectors or how to understand how your decisions can impact not only your own organization but individuals and society at large, then take a look at the courses that the international leadership development charity Common Purpose has to offer – they bring together leaders from the private, public and not-for-profit sectors.

We have discussed leadership, so now let us look at management.

Team dynamics

In an ideal world, you will have people with the right skills, style and experience filling the key roles within the organization. In reality, you often have a group of people in place and you have to discover their strengths and weaknesses and fit them into the most appropriate roles. People can surprise you – perhaps a move into an unexpected post will bring out the best in them. If your organization uses volunteers and lacks resources, like many charities, then getting all the right people in all the right places can be difficult but it is not impossible, and if your organization is to grow to its optimum potential, it is essential.

Remember this: The right people

Getting those who don't work well in the organization you are building to move on can be problematic, so it's important to use early assessment mechanisms so that if they do not work out, or will not, you can correct the recruitment mistakes that we all make before it's too late.

SHAPING YOUR TEAM

Initially, it is a good idea to take stock. Who have you got involved in the organization? What are their particular strengths and weaknesses and how do those qualities unite with your strategy for reaching your charity's goals? Try to match individuals with specific strengths with those who are weaker in these areas. Skills may exist in junior members of staff and volunteers that will also strengthen the team.

Quite apart from the specialists who are able to deliver your services, there are certain key functions that need to be fulfilled as a minimum, whatever the size of your charity. As a priority, you need someone who is good (and usually experienced) at dealing with figures who can administer the financial side of running a charity. As we saw in previous chapters, communicating with donors, handling their information and getting it into and managing databases is another key role. And, if the charity is to grow, you also need someone or a team dedicated to fundraising.

Of course, not everyone that you take on has to be a full-time, paid member of staff. You can look at other ways of getting certain roles and functions covered. For example, have you considered using volunteers, freelancers or interns? If you are talking about paid staff, do they need to be employees? Could you take advantage of the services of agency staff or a consultant who you can hire on a flexible, ad hoc basis?

Certainly, at the outset, you will need dedicated, diligent people on board because the workload nearly always demands more than their contractual hours, and they will need to be flexible because their role in an organization in its infancy is, of necessity, fluid. These individuals will be committed to your charity, and in return, you must be committed to them and their development. It is a fact of life that the people you take on in the early days of an organization are different from those who join an established charity later on.

Remember this: Fundraisers

Fundraising is a crucial function within the charity and although you may be at a stage of growth where you feel it is impossible to justify employing a fundraiser, you have to ask yourself, 'can you afford not to?' It is estimated that it takes about a year to recoup the cost of recruiting someone, and it's generally agreed that any fundraising team should eventually generate around five times its cost to the organization at least.

Remember this: Bookkeeper/accountant

If you only have enough funds to recruit one post, hire a bookkeeper or accountant. Getting the financial records in order from the outset is really important for the charity but also a legal necessity.

DEFINING TEAM ROLES

You have your inventory of the people in the organization and their qualities. Now you need to match them to a list of the necessary roles to be performed across the organization and what the person fulfilling each post is expected to do. Don't stop there – other details to include for each role include:

▶ What are they responsible and accountable for?

▶ Who will they report to?

▶ What relevant experience is required?

▶ How will their performance be measured?

▶ What remuneration/reward is appropriate?

Larger organizations may well have a human resources function, and so these job definitions will be more structured, but even very small, very new charities should look at role definitions and person specifications, because it will help you to recruit or move the right people into the right jobs, and help them to know what is expected of them.

Try it now

You may be struggling to come up with a definition of what you want from a role. If so, try looking at it another way – write a list of things that you don't want from that role.

MANAGING VOLUNTEERS

In many charities, volunteers are the lifeblood that allows them to operate on limited funds. Without those who are willing to give freely of their time and expertise, many charities would grind to a halt. Volunteers help because they believe in your mission and they want to make a difference. As soon as they feel their work is unappreciated or if the atmosphere is unwelcoming or uncomfortable, they will leave. So keeping your volunteers engaged and committed to your charity and being appreciative of their efforts is of paramount importance. You can make them feel fully involved, informed and appreciated by keeping them up-to-date with internal communications and thanking them for their contribution which really does make a difference.

Volunteers' activities need to be co-ordinated and supervised, and it is important that you make sure they have the appropriate skills for the tasks you are asking them to fulfil. Managing volunteers is notoriously difficult as many volunteers like to underline their non-employee and therefore non-conformist status. However, if you have created the right culture and your volunteers feel appreciated, they tend to be more reliable than you might think.

The role of volunteer co-ordinator should not be handed out lightly. If you consider that a volunteer co-ordinator may well be the first point of contact with the charity for someone wishing to support you or to volunteer, then clearly they have to not only represent your values but to be able to spot the potential in a good volunteer and work out how their skills might be appropriate. There are various training courses on offer from the Directory of Social Change and other providers on how to successfully manage a volunteer team and advice is also available on the NCVO website.

By the same token, don't forget training for the volunteers themselves. Perhaps their experience or skills are rusty and they need to be introduced to current practices, or maybe they need to better understand the culture and motivation of your charity if they are to do things the way that your charity likes them done.

What is clear is that all volunteers need to have clear guidelines on what they can do (a contract is not necessary though generally), they may need to be Criminal Records Bureau (CRB) checked and given special guidance before working with children or vulnerable adults, and they should be encouraged to claim out-of-pocket expenses at the agreed rates.

Try it now

Although people volunteer in order to support your cause, they are often looking to get something from the experience for themselves too. Whether it is to build confidence or to get relevant experience that will help them to gain a qualification/job, if you remember that they have needs too, it will be a healthier relationship. Treat them as you would a member of staff.

PROJECT CO-ORDINATORS

Sometimes there will be specific projects that your organization undertakes over and above your normal work. In this situation, it may be wise to create a temporary official post and to take on a co-ordinator for the sole purpose of moving the project forward. The person should have a relevant core knowledge base for this project and should be able to work to the budget. If you haven't already raised specific funding for the project, bid-writing experience would be useful. Project co-ordinators have to be self-motivated and work with minimum supervision as there may be no established chain of command for this post.

Students can be ideal candidates for special projects. You can contact your local university to find a student with the right skills who is perhaps looking for a part-time position, or a post-graduate intern, some of which have the added bonus of being academically supervised. Alternatively, you could look at a step scheme which provides students for short assignments and longer placements (see www.step.org.uk for example).

At Henshaws, we have used the MBA students of Manchester Business School for specific ten-week projects very successfully.

Culture

In the early days, you established your vision (what you want to achieve), your mission (how you plan to achieve it) and your values, which may well have covered things like integrity, excellence and efficiency.

The qualities are inexorably linked to the philosophy of your organization and hopefully the culture that people work in. They are however extremely difficult to quantify. As a charity, you exist to meet the needs of your beneficiaries and all those who work for the charity need to always keep in mind that they are working for this wider cause. This common cause can be a theme that helps to unify the team and create a culture in which everyone can be rightly proud of the work that you do. And service user groups provide essential feedback.

People sometimes remark to me that it must be fulfilling to work for a charity because 'you are doing something worthwhile' and because 'you must work with nice, like-minded people'. While the former is undoubtedly true, I'm not sure I subscribe to the latter statement. Certainly, at the birth of a charity, the people involved are often friends or people united by the same burning ambition to do something meaningful and helpful. However, once a charity is up and running and relatively well established, the staff you recruit may well care about the cause but they have the same foibles, concerns and failings as everyone else in any workplace. It is up to you to create a working environment that engenders loyalty and commitment, and that usually means committing in return to individual members of staff and making sure the individual members of the team complement each other's strengths and weaknesses.

When it comes to senior management teams, there has been a sea change of late within the sector. More and more charities are re-balancing the composition of the senior management team (SMT). While retaining the essence of why they exist, they are looking at a new, more commercially oriented way of operating – and that often means bringing in new staff to complement the existing talents and blend of skills. The chief executive is then required to work hard at the integration process, and at team development. You can employ methods such as away-days, performance evaluation and talent assessment and management exercises.

One word of caution – don't be fooled into thinking that all business procedures are the answer – many businesses are mediocre and what you are trying to build is a great charity.

Across the board, charities are looking at how they can retain high potential employees by developing their careers, rather than losing them to better-paid jobs in the private sector. Some are employing customized talent-management programmes, clear lines of professional development, and particularly for members of the SMT, appropriate succession plans.

You can also consider providing 'stretch assignments' to staff. These are tasks that are outside their normal comfort zone and current skills levels but that will help to prepare them for future advancement.

Here are some other methods that can help to bring out the very best in your staff and volunteers.

MOTIVATION

In terms of motivation, people working for a charity are no different from those who work in a commercial environment: everyone responds well to recognition, feeling valued, a sense of achievement, being given responsibility and opportunities for personal growth. In the charity sector, you have the added motivation of seeing your efforts benefiting the end-users too.

Other factors that affect motivation but are rarely taken into consideration include the culture of the working environment – you're aiming for a positive vibe, not negative but not too happy either; management – over-zealous and they feel stifled and are likely to under-perform, too little supervision and they may struggle; and remuneration – too little is definitely demotivating and gives a feeling of being undervalued but too much and you will not necessarily get a pro rata increase in performance.

If you are not sure about how to motivate your team, there are books and courses on the subject, or you could find a volunteer mentor who specializes in this area.

GOAL SETTING

One way to help staff to reach their potential is to set goals for them to achieve – how can they celebrate success if you have not qualified it for them? I suggest you get them involved in the goal-setting process so they have some sense of ownership. Together you can discuss how their personal goals are in harmony with the goals of the charity, as people are more motivated when they can see how their contribution is aiding the overall success of the organization.

Then, as a team, ask them what they think it is possible to achieve and what is needed to achieve the goal. If skills or training gaps are identified in the course of these discussions, this is something that you can hopefully address, budgets permitting. Once goals have been agreed, discuss and agree on how performance against goals will be measured.

ENCOURAGING TEAM PLAYERS

Even in a charity, human nature prevails and as your team grows in size, so too will rivalries, politics and competition. You do not want this to hamper the collective success of your organization or to detract from the work you are doing for your beneficiaries, so you may like to consider some of these practices to encourage team spirit and foster a good workplace atmosphere. Never underestimate the negative impact of office politics.

Remember this: Supportive culture

As your charity evolves, it is natural that you will out-grow some staff. It is to be expected but make sure your charity's culture lets people know that it's fine to move on if you feel out of your depth or that the job has overtaken you. The great thing is that more staff will thrive and surprise you and often themselves too.

Case study: Dr Rob Macmillan, Research Fellow, Third Sector Research Centre (TSRC)

Some years ago Colin Rochester likened the effort involved in managing and leading a small voluntary agency to 'juggling on a unicycle' (Rochester 1999, *Juggling on a Unicycle: a handbook for small voluntary agencies*, London, Centre for Voluntary Organisations, London School of Economics). This image captures very well the challenges of simultaneously reacting to and balancing multiple demands, with only limited resources, time and energy. Many fledgling and small voluntary organizations experience what is known more formally as the 'liability of smallness' (Rochester 2003: 116–119, 'The role of boards in small voluntary organisations', in C. Cornforth (ed) *The Governance of Public and Non-Profit Organisations: What do boards do?* London, Routledge). This is where small organizations can be vulnerable because they rely quite heavily on the commitment and range of skills of only a small number of people, including founder members. As a result they tend to focus on day-to-day tasks and activities. They have little time or space to engage with longer-term strategic planning, to understand the bigger picture, and to link up with other organizations or access external support. They are less visible and well known among key external stakeholders, and can thus lack legitimacy.

Hawthorn, a small and relatively new local project supporting vulnerable and disadvantaged young families, illustrates some of the challenges involved for organizations wishing to move beyond this scenario. It was founded by a committed community worker who identified a particular need in his local community. The project was run entirely by volunteers out of a church hall for several years, running informal drop in sessions for new parents and children. Committee members were recruited via word of mouth through informal networks, usually friends of the founder. Hawthorn was able to expand after becoming a charity and enjoying success in gaining a longer-term grant from a charitable trust. As a result it was able to employ its first two or three members of staff and offer more sessions. The founder became the paid manager. But it was now accountable to external funders as well as its users, and thus needed to become more formal and professional. Committee members now had responsibilities as trustees and as employers.

Mid-way through its period of grant funding Hawthorn entered a crisis, in which its liabilities of smallness became apparent. Trustees were concerned that the paid manager was not creating the systems needed and building the external relationships required for a well led and run voluntary organization. He preferred the informal ethos and hands-on project work associated with Hawthorn's first few years, and seemed reluctant to share day-to-day information and to think ahead for the longer term. The trustees commissioned an independent organizational audit. This revealed some strategic and operational shortcomings and recommended the development of clearer systems and a strategic plan. Eventually the manager left quite suddenly, and Hawthorn was thrown into turmoil with differing perspectives, strained relationships and torn loyalties built out of longstanding friendships. Much of the essential information about running the organization, including key contacts, was in the manager's head rather than written down. Yet the organization was still responsible for running services and reporting to its funders. Its external reputation was in doubt, and for a while it faced the prospect of closure.

Moving forward three years and Hawthorn is in a much stronger position. Its grant funding is drawing to a close and it is seeking replacement funding. But it is now also bidding for a contract from the local council; something inconceivable just a couple of years before. It has a much clearer structure and set of activities, with clearer role descriptions and boundaries between users, volunteers, staff and trustees. It has rebranded, can demonstrate what it does, and has a more credible outcome related story to tell of the difference it can make to vulnerable young families. It has a business plan and is involved in strategic discussions around family support in the locality. Looking back, the key factor in the organization's survival through crisis was the leadership provided by the board of trustees, and particularly the chair.

At the height of the crisis the trustees decided to stick together and stand by the organization. Over subsequent months the chair took on a much more active role and stable presence, supporting remaining staff and volunteers, and liaising openly with funders. A new, relatively inexperienced manager was recruited and tasked with developing the systems and strategies required for a more professionally-run organization: to put it back on track. With active support from the chair, and some mentoring support, she has rebuilt Hawthorn from a particularly low point.

Of course, dilemmas have arisen and challenges remain in Hawthorn's journey, as with running any voluntary organization. These include, for example, how the sensitive ecology of relationships among staff and volunteers changes as people come and go; how the respective roles of the chair and co-ordinator are continuously negotiated over time; whether Hawthorn is in a strong enough position to compete for contracts in a changing commissioning environment, and whether the organization has had to become almost too structured, losing some of its informal accessibility as a result. What has been a noticeable legacy of the crisis, however, has been ongoing attention to the culture of the organization, and in particular a remarkable willingness to confront difficult issues before they have more damaging consequences.

This case study was produced by the Third Sector Research Centre (TSRC) from its 'Real Times' long-term qualitative research programme examining third sector organizations and activities over time. For more information on this and other research programmes from TSRC, see www.tsrc.ac.uk. In order to protect the anonymity of research participants, the organization has been given a pseudonym, and some relevant details have been changed.

Focus points

Good leadership is not the same as good management.

You are aiming to have people with the right skills filling the key roles.

The people you take on in the early stages of your charity have different skills from those required of the people who join later.

It is important to define roles and expectations.

Volunteers form a vital part of charity teams.

Achieving a positive and appreciative culture in the organization engenders loyalty and commitment, and staff retention.

Good communication is key.

Next step

Much of what we have discussed in this chapter, especially regarding motivation and team pruning, come under the auspices of human resources, which is a specialist field, and one that we will look at in closer detail in the next chapter.

10

Looking after your people

In this chapter you will learn:

▸ *How to handle change management*
▸ *About the importance of codes of best practice and codes of conduct*
▸ *The ins and outs of insurance for charities*
▸ *Whether you need insurance for the sphere of operation for your charity*

Just like the marketing manager, many HR directors in the charity sector have a suspicion that their role is not as valued as that of the Finance Director, for example. In light of the fact that your staff are your greatest asset, that is not altogether fair.

One of the problems for HR is that lots of people think they know how to do it, so they don't need to hire a professional. In reality, of course, it is a skilled profession that requires a lot of training and experience, particularly in the implementation and interpretation of employment law. By consulting your HR provision *before* taking big decisions on things such as a change programme, it could save you a big headache further down the line. Your HR specialist should be able to tell you if you are heading into a problematic situation – and they can usually advise on the various options available to you. Ultimately, if you are serious about your staff being central to your organization's goals, HR can make that so much easier to achieve. HR can also play a key role in gaining staff feedback and encouraging them to contribute as much as they can.

Having a human resource function may appear to be a luxury that only the larger charities can afford, but the issues that the HR department deals with are common to charities of all shapes and size, and these time-consuming potential personnel problems must be dealt with by someone. However, personnel issues often get side-lined in smaller charities in preference for funding and fundraising, IT and infrastructure.

Whether you have an HR person to look at these issues or it falls to someone in the senior management team, it is worth giving serious consideration to the following personnel topics because, although they may seem like a low priority, when things go wrong, it can be a time-consuming and costly exercise to put them right.

Employment relations

There is strong evidence that positive employee relations lead to greater commitment, engagement and better performance, not just of the individual but of the organization as a whole.

Although this workplace relationship is often guided by HR, it is the skill and enthusiasm of individual line managers that have the greatest influence on whether or not employee engagement works. So support for, and development of, line managers by HR is important.

There are various practices that you can employ to build employee engagement. They include:

▶ Employee involvement – methods such as direct communication with staff consultation groups and recognizing individual employee contribution

▶ Team-working – see Chapter 9

▶ Work-life balance – policies on work-life balance are being used by employers to underpin positive workplace behaviours. Various surveys by the Chartered Institute of Personnel and Development (CIPD) underline the link between work-life balance, commitment and performance. Many charity bosses strongly support work-life initiatives such as flexible working and an informal workplace climate, and accept that in light of the lower salaries paid in the sector, then every effort should be made to support staff.

One of the most vital ingredients for employee engagement is effective communication. Communication is very much about developing the organization's culture, which should be one of the central roles of the HR function but, as I mentioned in Chapter 9, this has to start at the top with good leadership. Success depends upon the existence of a consistent, clear strategy linked to a shared understanding of the purpose of the charity. Communication cannot be seen as a 'top down' exercise. Two-way dialogue is needed so that people have a meaningful opportunity to feed their views upwards and to have input into improving organizational performance. Staff consultation must be taken seriously and developed over a period of time. Don't forget the opportunities provided by new social media channels to create dialogue and engagement.

Remember this: Managing workplace conflict

The role most commonly associated with HR is their mediation function – ability to manage conflict and resolve workplace issues. Mediation has taken the emphasis away from formal disciplinary action and grievance procedures, although sadly this is still a necessity on occasions.

Change management

With the difficult economic climate and modernization of work practices, the charity sector is undergoing unprecedented change and many charities have had to adapt through organizational change in order to survive.

According to the Chartered Institute of Personal Development (CIPD), organizations across all sectors undergo a major change at least once every three years, but over 40 per cent of reorganizations fail to meet their stated objectives.

All changes that affect the staff need to be handled sensitively and decisively, especially redundancy programmes, restructuring and cultural change programmes. Statistically, the charity sector attracts a disproportionate number of employment tribunal cases, so the need for care is evident.

Most successful change management comes down to simply keeping staff informed. When staff know what is happening and why, they are more likely to embrace the change. Staff consultation involves hearing back from employees, and can also ease change as it helps to make it more relevant and to give all those affected a sense of involvement. And people do not simply want to know how change is going to affect them – they are also concerned about what impact the changes might have on the mission. If they can see how change might build on the charity's values, it is easier to understand and accept.

Remember this: Motivational change

Change is always unsettling, but change that doesn't seem to have any obvious purpose is worse. Always communicate to your employees what's going on and why if you want to keep them on-side.

Competence or competency framework

Having a competency framework in place will help individual members of staff to understand what behaviours and actions will be valued and recognized by your charity and what are the expected areas and levels of performance that you want from them.

In the past, HR professionals have tended to draw a clear distinction between 'competences' and 'competencies'. The term 'competence' (competences) was used to describe what people need to do to perform a job and was concerned with effect and output rather than effort and input. 'Competency' (competencies) described the behaviour that lies behind competent performance, such as critical thinking or analytical skills, and described what people bring to the job. However, in recent years, there has been growing awareness that job performance requires a mix of behaviour, attitude and action and hence the two terms are now more often used interchangeably.

When setting up a competency framework, your HR team should take care to only include measurable components, generally aiming for no more than 12 for any particular role (and preferably fewer). Getting the degree of detail of a framework right can be tricky – too broad and it won't give enough guidance; too detailed and instead of being helpful, it becomes overly bureaucratic and time-consuming.

A rough guideline for titles to include in a competency framework might be:

▶ People management

▶ Team skills

▶ Communication skills

▶ Results-orientation

▶ Problem-solving

▶ Customer service skills.

If used correctly, a competency policy can help to manage and monitor performance and development but it can also play a key role in any change management process by setting out new organizational requirements. And, of course, it has become a useful tool in recruitment because it enables recruiters to assess against a clear range of criteria and behaviours.

To ensure the framework is most effective, managers should be trained in how to get the most from it and there should be clear links between the needs of the job and what your charity is aiming to achieve in terms of skills, experience and behaviours. A good competency framework should contain a mix of job-specific and organization-specific behaviours and reflect the need to build a diverse workforce, a broad talent base and complementary team roles.

Try it now
When using the framework, it's important to recognize an individual's potential to develop certain competencies.

Remember this: Staff representation
Trustees also have a key role in setting the values and ensuring that the staff are representing these values.

Code of good governance

All chief executives run their charity in their own style, putting the emphasis where they see fit. However, the received wisdom on the way to run your charity in the most effective and efficient way possible has been collected together by the Association of Chief Executives of Voluntary Organizations and published. The Good Governance guide offers advice on the principles of good governance and it was drafted by the voluntary sector, for the sector. It is now in its second edition.

The code outlines six high-level principles that apply to voluntary and community organizations of all type and size. The code says, 'Underlying each principle is the additional principle of equality – that of ensuring equality, diversity and equality of treatment for all section of the community.' The six principles are as follows.

An effective board can provide good governance and leadership by:

▶ Understanding their role and responsibilities – especially in relation to legal duties, the stewardship of assets, the provisions of the governing document, the external environment and the total structure of the organization.

▶ Ensuring delivery of organizational purposes of aims – by ensuring they remain relevant and valid, developing long-term strategy, agreeing operational plans and budgets, monitoring progress, evaluating results, assessing outcomes and impact, reviewing and/or amending the plan and budget if appropriate.

▶ Working effectively both as individuals and a team – this could be through recruiting new board members with the skills, experience and diversity to meet the organization's changing needs, providing induction to new members, offering opportunities for training and development, and reviewing performance.

▶ Exercising effective control – by ensuring that the organization understands and complies with legal and regulatory requirements, that it has good internal financial and management controls, that it regularly reviews the major risks, and that delegation to committees, staff and volunteers works effectively.

▶ Behaving with integrity – by safeguarding and promoting the organization's reputation, acting according to high ethical standards, identifying and managing conflicts of interest and loyalty, maintaining independence of decision making, and delivering impact that best meets the needs of beneficiaries.

▶ Being open and accountable – including open communications, informing people about the organization and its work, appropriate consultation on significant changes to its services or policies, listening and responding to the views of supporters, funders, beneficiaries, service users and other interested parties, handling complaints constructively, impartially and effectively, and considering the organization's responsibilities to the wider community, for example, its environmental impact.

All of the above principles are expanded upon in the report which was jointly formulated by the Association of Chief Executives of Voluntary Organizations (ACEVO), the Charity Commission, Charity Trustee Networks (CTN), the Institute of Chartered Secretaries and Administrators (ICSA) and the National Council for Voluntary Organizations (NCVO) and is available from their websites.

Try it now

The Health and Safety Executive (HSE) offers a wide variety of publications and advice on health and safety issues for staff, managers and the general public (www.hse.gov.uk). It is part of the HR function to make sure they are up to speed on the topic, but in the absence of an HR person, you need to keep abreast of developments yourself.

Insuring your charity

Insurance is sometimes seen as a costly burden for charities but charity insurance claims are more common than you might think – 20 per cent of charities claimed on their insurance in the last year – and without the right cover in place, you could be left exposed to costly payouts.

If injury or damage does occur, and your organization is responsible, a claim could be made against you. If the claim is successful, you would be liable for paying compensation unless you are insured.

It is the responsibility of the trustees to protect the charity's assets and resources. Insurance is one of the most appropriate ways of protecting the charity against loss, damage or liability and, after proper assessment, the right level of insurance should be taken. If you don't have a human resources officer to advise you and the board, you can seek advice on these matters from an insurance agent found through the British Insurance Brokers' Association (www.biba.org.uk) or the NCVO's publication *Getting the Best Insurance Deal* is available from their website.

Fortunately, you are allowed to pay for insurance using charity funds but, if it is specific trustee indemnity insurance (TII) to protect trustees personally from having to pay legal claims, this must be bought out of the trustee's own pocket, as you should not use charity funds for TII. Where charity trustees have acted honestly and reasonably, they are in any event entitled to an indemnity from the charity's assets for any liabilities incurred by them as trustees.

PROFESSIONAL INDEMNITY INSURANCE

If your charity provides a professional service, such as counselling, sharing specialist advice and information or teaching skills, whether for a fee or otherwise, you could be liable if this is provided negligently, so professional indemnity insurance to cover against claims could well be worth considering.

PUBLIC LIABILITY INSURANCE

If your organization comes into contact with the public (beneficiaries, volunteers, non-members and other organizations), you must consider buying public liability insurance. This cover protects your organization against claims which could be made against you for accidental damage to property and compensation for accidental injury to third parties, where you may be at fault.

LEGAL EXPENSES INSURANCE

This might seem like an unnecessary expense, but in such changing times and with employment tribunals on the increase, having legal expenses insurance can be useful. This form of insurance usually covers the costs of any employment dispute and your liability for compensation awarded to an employee. It can also help to prevent time-wasters who feel they have nothing to lose if they take their employer through the legal system.

Remember this: Insuring employees

If your charity employs staff, you are required by law to buy employers' liability insurance. If you use volunteers, for insurance purposes, you should treat them the same way as staff. And, it scarcely needs saying but, if your charity owns or operates any vehicles – mini-buses, delivery vans, etc. – legally, you must have motor insurance.

Try it now

Before organizing any big fundraising events such as concerts, galas, shows or fetes, it is worth looking into taking out cover against losses arising from cancellation due to bad weather, as your up-front costs can be considerable. You should definitely investigate public liability insurance for major events.

Case study: Fran Scott, HR and Governance Executive at The Outward Bound Trust

The Outward Bound Trust is an educational charity and is the UK's leading provider of bursary-assisted outdoor learning. It aims to help young people through learning and adventure in the wild, helping them to build resilience and preparing them to face the future with confidence. In 70 years it has positively influenced the lives of more than a million young people. The Trust employs just over 250 staff split between six centres, a Head Office in Cumbria, and a fundraising office in London. Instructors make up just over half of the staffing levels, with the rest split between Educational Sales, Business Development, Fundraising, Administration, Finance, Business Support and Marketing.

When I came into this role in August 2012 it was a new post for The Outward Bound Trust. The Trust's strategic framework for 2012–2017, 'Each Adventure a New Beginning' has a strong focus on supporting staff excellence, with a commitment to increase staff engagement, give staff a clearer sense of professional development, develop management skills, improve the ways we work together and keep the strategy alive by improving internal communications and embedding the strategy in HR related processes.

This has given the HR role a very clear focus, with the establishment of an 'Employee Advisory Group' made up of elected reps from across the trust, and subsequent consultation with them on the introduction of a new appraisal system and a trust-wide induction course. Management development workshops have been developed to help with people management skills, and further training is planned. A competency framework is being developed, linked to salary structure, to give a clearer development path for staff, and this is partly in response to a request through the Employee Advisory Group that the trust should seek a way to move those staff currently on minimum wage onto a 'living wage' salary.

In comparison with the public and private sector organizations I have worked for in the past, my experience of working within the voluntary sector is that the HR role in a charity tends to be a very wide-ranging role. Many charities are fairly small organizations and therefore often choose not to have a specific HR role, as The Outward Bound Trust had done until 2012, or where they do, it is an entirely generalist role encompassing the traditional personnel admin and management, organizational development, recruitment, reward & benefits, learning & development, and often a bit of health & safety, or in my case, governance thrown in with the job as well.

I have found that the emphasis here has been very much on the organizational development end of the role, with a clear remit to support the strategy of the trust in terms of building engagement and making it an organization which people aspire to work for, are motivated to excel, and want to stay for the longer term. Traditionally outdoor education is a sector with relatively high turnover of staff and The Outward Bound Trust has made concerted and focused efforts to increase the length of service of our instructors. Between 2007 and 2012 this has increased from 3 years to 5 years, creating the most stable and best qualified cohort of instructors in the trust's history. This ongoing work has been achieved by the focused and systematic improvement to our salary structure, provision of meaningful training and development opportunities and seeking ever improving ways to communicate effectively with staff.

The culture of developing effective managers, good communication and staff engagement, are combined with the natural advantage of many charities: the fact that often people choose to work for a particular charity because they 'believe in' what it stands for or does. Levels of discretionary effort are high across the trust and there is a high degree of commitment to doing an excellent job. This is further encouraged by a strong emphasis on rewarding these efforts, and this year an employee nominated award, 'The Chairman's Award', was established to recognize and reward those who have made an outstanding contribution to delivering any aspect of our strategy. This has built on a general culture, led by senior management, and encouraged throughout the trust of seeking out opportunities to recognize and celebrate excellence. www.outwardbound.org.uk

Focus points

HR can help to make your staff central to your goals, as their approach characterizes the values of your organization.

HR personnel have the skills to orchestrate better employment relations and to train line managers to be more effective in employee engagement.

Change management tends to go more smoothly with the central involvement of co-ordination.

HR should be instrumental in the formulation of a competency framework.

A good governance code helps the board to ensure the charity is run effectively and efficiently.

Advising on insurance for your charity is an integral part of the HR function.

Next step

In the next chapter, we will follow on from some of the themes raised above to explore risk management.

11

Storm-proofing your charity

In this chapter you will learn:

▶ *Why risk management is important*
▶ *How to assess risk*
▶ *The current dangers of pension liabilities to charities*
▶ *How to limit trustee liability*

It is not just charities who are finding it tough at the moment. The whole of the British economy is struggling and if your charity is to avoid being shipwrecked in these stormy seas, there are certain preventative measures that it is wise to take.

In an effort to help trustees to navigate these treacherous waters, the Charity Commission is offering guidance on how to review an organization's operations. This risk assessment framework offers a checklist of 15 questions that cover the four broad categories of strategy, financial health, governance and making best use of resources (the full list can be found on the Charity Commission's website). If you pay special attention to these areas, you should manage to stay off the rocks.

Risk management

Before we look at those four key areas, it helps to establish what we mean by risk assessment and risk management and its importance. Understanding the risks your charity faces is at the heart of your governance, operational viability and planning.

No matter how diligent you are in formulating your financial and funding plans, things change and plans do not always work out as you had foreseen. One single change can then have a knock-on effect so that the whole plan is off-course or fails completely.

Risk management is not about avoiding risks but about understanding them, being better able to deal with issues, and better informed to make decisions should the need arise. As a result, you can avoid unforeseen costs, delays or potential damage to your reputation in the worst case scenarios.

In most charities, the trustees set the parameters of the risk identification and management process and they are responsible for review, but it is the staff that performs the actual task of risk assessment and management, sometimes with the help of professional advisers, although the Finance Director usually takes the lead.

WHERE TO START

You can look at the four key areas highlighted by the Charity Commission and methodically work through the organization, starting with a strategic assessment and then moving on to the financial assessment until eventually all of the four main areas and every department in the organization should be covered.

In each case, you first have to define the risk you wish to consider, what might cause it, what the impact might be and what is the likelihood of it occurring. From that point, you can work out how you might prevent that risk or limit its impacts. Of course, there may be more than one cause or impact but the principle remains the same. An example might illustrate the formula more clearly. So you define the risk as being that 'you will not have enough funding to run a certain type of operational delivery'. The cause might be 'that the funding bid for the work was inadequately written' and the impact of this is 'that the delivery has to be cancelled'. I would then name this risk as 'Poor bid applications' so you can distinguish it from other assessments and you can easily identify them on a list.

Once you have identified the risk and its possible causes, it is easier to reduce the chances of it occurring, even if you cannot prevent it entirely. Identifying possible impacts helps you to plan action to limit the damage in the event that it happens. And finally, the last thing you have to add to the mix is the chance of it happening within a given timeframe.

Once you have established this assessment framework, you can then decide what risk is acceptable or can be dealt with on a day-to-day basis, and what decisions need to be referred immediately to the trustee board.

The difficulty is developing a reporting system within the management structure and for the trustees. This usually involves the development of a risk register, which covers: the risks, the impact, the probability, whose responsibility it is, what controls are in place, what assurance is available on the effectiveness of these controls, actions that have been taken, actions that are going to be taken and how and when are they going to be reviewed.

Remember this: Timescale

Unless you define the period of time that your risk assessment covers, it is meaningless. For example, when considering whether the UK is likely to be hit by a serious hurricane in the next few years, the risk is low. If you extend that time period to the next 10,000 years, then the risk is considerably higher. The same applies to the risks you are assessing in your organization. When assessing a business risk, look at a specified period, for example a financial year or three years; if it's a project, the duration of the project is probably the best idea.

Try it now

If the prospect of applying a risk assessment plan to your whole organization is too daunting and you simply don't know where to start, break it down into smaller, more manageable blocks. So start with a single department or project and in this way, you are not trying to solve all the problems at once.

STRATEGY

Firstly, it is useful to compare what your charity is up to with your core charitable aims – do they match up? One significant risk is to find yourself operating outside of your charitable object. Ask yourselves whether any shift has been intentional or as a result of operational drift. Of course, the litmus test is whether or not these activities present any risks. For example, as a result of this shift in focus, has there been an impact on funding opportunities, either now or in the future? Will it affect demand for services?

Bear in mind that you don't always have to consider it as being a negative. Sometimes change can herald new opportunities and these should be assessed as well.

Larger charities should have Audit Committees that review processes and risk. It is important that Trustees and management keep a record of how risk was evaluated, when and by whom.

FINANCIAL HEALTH

The current economic climate is having an impact on us all and never has it been more important to monitor your charity's financial health and to be confident that you can sustain your operations in the short to medium term. You should be asking yourselves, can we meet all our contractual obligations and commitments when they fall due? Have we explored all the funding, income generation and fundraising opportunities and spread and sources?

In order to assess the risks, you and the trustee board need to be abreast of your finances, cash flow forecasts, fundraising strategies, debts and investments, and to identify biggest risk areas. The best way to do this might be to set up working groups to look into key areas of major liability such as investments, pensions or mortgages, and to report back to the board. In this way, you are actively managing risk.

▶ Cash flow

Cash is the lifeblood of any organization and many flourishing organizations including charities come to grief because of cash flow problems – running out of cash is a major risk. You can have any number of funding and fundraising promises and countless contracts down the line but, if you cannot afford to pay operational costs or your debts as they fall due, you have to stop operating immediately.

Even if it feels like your fundraisers are having lots of successes, there is inevitably a gap between incurring costs and being paid what you have been pledged/promised.

The aim with cash flow is to strike a balance between making your money work for your charity by investing in deposit accounts or short-term investments and ensuring that you have enough cash available to pay for the day-to-day running expenses of the organization plus any outgoings such as new IT equipment, etc.

Some of the ways suggested by the NCVO to help you to manage your cash flow more effectively include:

▶ Tactfully getting prompt payment from debtors

▶ Centralize payments and streamline procedures for different functional areas such as accounts payable and payroll, by using BACS payment methods, for example

- Choose banks that can offer customized cash management services such as handling appeal monies

- Using budgets and strategic plans, make your cash flow forecasting more accurate

- Review the cash situation regularly to ensure balances approximate to those in the budget and investigate any significant discrepancies

- Telephone and internet banking can be quicker and cheaper

- Make sure all financial transactions are properly authorized at every level in order to avoid any improper use of the organization's cash.

If you have a cash flow crisis, this is when you might need to fall back on your reserves policy which can help you to ride out the weeks or months of deficit. You may not consider cash flow enough of an emergency to dip into your reserves, but if it threatens your ability to pay salaries or to deliver services that is probably reason enough to use reserves, which can be topped back up in brighter times.

And, if you find yourselves in the fortunate position of having liquidity in the long term, you have choices – you can invest in easy-access bank savings accounts, you can plough money back into the charity to help it grow or broaden expertise or, depending on the amount, you could look at long-term investments.

Remember this: Cash flow

When planning how much working capital you will need for the coming year, always add 25 per cent to the figure you arrive at. In this way, you have some leeway so that small set-backs won't scupper you financially.

Try it now

When putting together your cash flow projections, did you remember to include employment costs such as National Insurance contributions (can add around 11 per cent to your wage bill), VAT and often overlooked costs such as business rates, insurance and training?

▶ Pension debt

Pensions liability currently represents a major financial risk for many charities, especially those who find themselves with multi-employer defined-benefit pension schemes as they are exposed to the biggest problems. This is because the schemes agree to pay staff an agreed amount (a defined benefit) when they retire. Investments have been underperforming and so there is a gap – a liability – between the investments and the benefits promised. This gap remains the liability of the organizations involved. These include local authority schemes or schemes run by a national charity with independent local affiliates, such as YMCA's and Age UK's, and some Pensions Trust schemes.

These multi-employer schemes are extremely difficult to quit. And, when a charity's final employee leaves the scheme, the charity then faces a 'cessation liability', whereby it must find the entire deficit immediately.

And if you think it won't actually happen, think again. The Hirwaun YMCA ran into difficulties last year when the last employees in the pension scheme retired, meaning that the charity had to make up the shortfall in their contributions. In their case, the Chair of Hirwaun YMCA, Colin Shaw, was personally liable for £18,200 and was being sued by the YMCA Pension Plan Trustee. The entire pension plan is £29m in deficit and was closed to new entrants in 2007. At time of writing, Shaw has said that he expected his organization, the Hirwaun YMCA, would have to sell its building and close down next year in order to pay the pension debt.

And this is not an isolated case. Many charities now face a real risk of closure due to pension debt, while many others are being forced to divert donations and fundraising monies to pay for growing pensions debts.

This is a major liability that trustees should be monitoring very closely. The risk management of pension liability is crucial, especially if you are part of a multi-employer pension scheme. Major charities are now lobbying the pensions minister to ask for changes in the rules to address the problems that face so many charities of all sizes, and requesting a support fund 'to allow charities to borrow money to pay off their pension deficits and then pay the borrowed money back over an agreed period of time.'

Under existing rules, the charities that are continuing with the threat of closure hanging over them because of pension debts are known as 'zombie charities' because they are effectively 'the walking dead'.

Many charities have or are moving towards defined contribution schemes. They pay an amount to individuals on retirement relative to the performance of the investment, and therefore there is no gap to be filled.

Trustees can freeze when it comes to risk management of pensions but burying your head and hoping it will go away is not the answer. If you are a new or small charity, you can act well before pension debt becomes a problem. For those who have existing pension schemes, the trustees need to make sure that they know the true extent of liabilities and give serious and immediate thought to how to manage the risk. Auto-enrolment does not necessarily increase the risk; it may however significantly increase the organization's ongoing pension contribution.

▶ Investments

Part of the financial risk management strategy will mean routinely assessing whether the investment of surplus money and reserve funds is being put to suitable use. Not all funds will necessarily be ploughed into making a financial return – some might be a programme-related investment to further your charity's aims. Moreover, when investing for financial return, you need to assess what level of investment risk you are prepared to take and then how you divide up the funds between high, medium and low risk investments. Diversity is usually the key, but professional advice is the best way forward, whether you then manage the investments yourself or appoint a professional investment manager is up to you. There are a whole host of investment advisers who specialize in the charity sector.

Many charities will have an investment committee to regularly review the performances and level of risk of the investments.

Governance

Your trustee board should collectively have the skills, knowledge and experience to meet current and future needs. Given the demands of the economic downturn on funding sources and the possible ensuing changes to your activities, you need to check that this is still the case. Getting the right trustees on the board whose skills and experience can help you to weather the current and future rough seas is prudent risk management. Also, during these hard times, your board may want to meet more frequently, to delegate the review of risk to various sub-groups, and to work more closely together on particular subjects.

The trustee board should consider reviewing its procedures regarding fraud and to make certain its controls are robust enough to prevent fraud, as it is proven that the risks of fraud increase during an economic downturn. Perhaps a review would be in order at a time when the pressures to commit fraud are high and the ways to do so are so widely available and diverse.

Remember this: Reporting

Trustees are required to make a risk management statement in their trustees' annual report if the charity is above the audit threshold, but it is good practice for trustees of smaller charities to do the same, even if the charity falls below the audit threshold and it is not a legal requirement.

Try it now

Together with the trustee board, you should establish a disaster recovery plan that enables your charity to resume normal or near normal service to your beneficiaries if a serious incident occurs, for example, failure of IT systems, which prevents you from operating as usual.

UNINCORPORATED RISK TO TRUSTEES

A key area of governance that needs a risk management review is the risk of your charity remaining unincorporated.

If yours is a charitable company or a CIO, then your trustees are afforded a degree of liability protection, with the primary liability falling upon the charity/corporate vehicle, not the trustees personally. However, trustees of unincorporated charities are personally liable.

As part of the risk management framework for governance, it is important that trustees fully understand their liability and do their due diligence. Although it is rare in practice for trustees of unincorporated organizations to become liable for the charity's debts, it is very important for trustees to be aware that they are liable. One way for trustees to protect themselves from liability, if they wish for the charity to remain unincorporated, is to take out indemnity insurance but it does not cover all eventualities – it is much better to get the charity status sorted out properly.

Making best use of resources

This may not seem like an obvious area of risk but even the smallest weakness can balloon into a major problem if left unattended in this current climate. So, when reviewing your organization's activities and resources with a view to risk management, you need to satisfy yourself that you are getting the most out of them.

Are you maximizing the many financial benefits that come with being a charitable organization? For example, have you claimed the maximum gift aid available? If you claimed more frequently, would you avert the risk of cash flow problems? Have you investigated every avenue of tax relief and used them to full effect? What about using a trading subsidiary to maximize tax allowances?

And don't forget that your staff come under the title of resources. Perhaps a review of the suitability of current staff resources and skills mix would be timely. Are you utilizing your volunteers at optimum efficiency? Would a volunteer co-ordinator be a worthwhile investment if they are currently being under used?

Turning adversity into a positive

It is a given, especially in difficult economic times, that all charities should regularly assess and review the risks they face in all areas of their work and plan for the management of those risks, because if your risk register is just a rarely visited set of tick boxes, an unexpected event could cause paralysis in your organization. On the contrary, a robust risk management process will allow you to assess how your assets and resources can be protected and put to best use. Nonetheless, things sometimes go wrong. Hopefully, your risk management planning will help you to deal with any crisis calmly, effectively and with expediency.

At the same time, try to remember that some crises can be turned into a positive for you, if approached the right way. What you want to do is to avoid a disaster or mishap creating bad PR for you among your supporters. For example, if a horse-riding adventure at a council-run location for disabled children has to be cancelled, don't wait for disappointed parents to approach the media saying how you have let down their children. Instead, react swiftly with a press release saying how disappointed you are that cuts in local authority spending have resulted in the closure of this course and how great the course had been for and what a difference it had made to your beneficiaries. Telling your story with a positive emphasis may well encourage your donors to do more of a good thing and want to help you further.

Try it now

Risk management should be present in every part of your organization. Make sure everyone knows how to play their part in managing risk.

Remember this: Be flexible

Have a risk management policy of course, but don't put all your faith in processes and mechanisms – you can't avoid all risk – you just have to manage it and react quickly and positively when things go wrong.

Case study: Dr Linda Spedding, legal adviser and governance expert

The cornerstones of good charity governance in my view are ethical conduct, honesty, legal compliance, transparency and integrity, coupled with proper reporting and communication to and with all relevant stakeholders including sponsors. Charities and voluntary organizations hold money on trust for others and must keep proper books sufficient to show the financial position at any point in time. In particular, if the books are not kept in order there is a high risk of restricted funds being misapplied and the trustees being in breach of the law. Accounts must be fully compliant with the SORP format: there are no other options.

I consider that the Statement of Recommended Practice on Accounting and Reporting by Charities (SORP 2000) – a standard approved by the Accounting Standards Board that applies to all of Britain and Ireland (including the Republic) – has become one of the most important requirements that a governing body should be aware of. This has impacted dramatically upon the operation of charities and the responsibilities of trustees. As a result it has had legal repercussions as regards risk management for trustees, even for relatively small charitable organizations. In particular funding institutions, service users and the Charity Commission are more vigilant in this era of corporate and social governance.

As has been made clear in other sectors – such as in the private sector with the Turnbull guidance for listed companies – risk management must occur at board level. For charities some brainstorming at board level should take place to identify and prioritise the risks that the charity might face. The Charity Commission has stated that it does not expect template risk reporting from charities but some system to indicate that they have taken on board a style of management that has assessed the risks. An example would be to analyse the risks into categories of probability such as from 1 to 5 and then deal with the impact. A risk could be:

✳ High probability but low impact (e.g. old office equipment fails);
✳ Low probability but high impact (e.g. threat of violence to volunteers from poor security equipment); and
✳ High probability and high impact (e.g. health and safety risks from faulty equipment).

Failure to do anything may trigger a non-compliance letter from the Charity Commission. Charities should consider what would happen in a disaster, such as if they were to lose all of their records. Trustees, management and staff should be involved in an ongoing risk management process.

The overall objective of SORP is to make accounting standards true and fair and to restrict the possibility of dubious practices. A charity must now present its annual accounts in a certain format. Funds received over the period must be analysed into restricted and unrestricted funds.

▶ Restricted funds

Clearly all funds received by a charitable group are restricted as regards the general restriction that any charity must spend its money in accordance with its charitable objectives. A charity cannot spend money on anything it was not established to do, however worthy the cause.

In addition there are more specific restrictions. If someone donates for a particular purchase such as the purchase of a particular item then that is how it must be spent. Should it prove impossible to spend the money for that purpose then the money must be returned to the donor unless they give permission for the money to be used in another way.

Under charity law restricted funds must be accounted for separately in accordance with SORP. The SORP also requires trustees to include in their annual report a statement confirming that the major risks, to which the charity is exposed, as identified by the trustees, have been reviewed and systems have been established to mitigate those risks.

Dr Spedding (www.lindaspedding.co.uk) has been passionate about assisting the community – local, national and international – and understands the key tasks and personal qualities required for representing charities or foundations, including, in particular, proper governance.

Throughout her professional life she has carried out pro bono work and assisted ethnic minority charities assisting women, children and the handicapped in particular. She also works on substantive legal and lifestyle issues of women in law and launched the Women in Law service www.womeninlaw.com and www.womeninlawinternational.com.

Focus points

All charities need a risk assessment framework and risk management policies in place.

The processes should be applied to every aspect of your charity but start with strategy and work methodically through the organization.

The financial health of your charity needs greater risk management in this difficult and unpredictable economic climate.

Pension debt can close charities.

The governing body itself needs risk assessment to make sure it's in good shape to make informed decisions about risk management.

Review whether your charity is making the best use of its resources.

Despite planning, you cannot avoid all risk. Be flexible enough to react swiftly and efficiently if disaster strikes and where possible, turn a negative into a positive.

Next step

When compiling and reviewing your organization's risk assessments, you might want to see if there are other organizations with similar purposes which may be open to collaboration and joint working. This can result in greater efficiency for both charities, and may pave the way towards greater partnership or even a merger, and we will discuss this in the next chapter.

12

Partnerships and mergers

In this chapter you will learn:

▶ *About the advantages of collaborating with other charities*
▶ *When merging with another charity is a good option*
▶ *How to make a merger successful*
▶ *When to think about winding up your charity.*

Running a small- to medium-sized charity can be quite an isolating experience and in the current climate, some charities are finding it a daily struggle to stay afloat, but what motivates them to keep going is the desire to provide the best possible service to those who benefit from their work.

Many charities, irrespective of size, are discovering that by working together with other charities in the same field, they are able to operate more efficiently, to share the costs and, in some cases, to deliver better co-ordinated services – plus you have the benefit of a network of people you can talk to.

The extension of collaborating with other charities is when two charities link or merge together to become one, and this too has its merits, both in terms of efficiency, sharing resources and saving money.

Collaborating with another charity

By co-ordinating your resources with another charity, you may find that you are able to operate more economically and your beneficiaries can often benefit too from joined-up services with each charity using their specialism. We saw in Chapter 6 on funding how charities can join forces to win bigger contracts to deliver public services that they would not have been able to win on their own, for example.

The Government and funders in general want charities to work together so that they have fewer organizations to deal with and they know that support costs are being minimized.

Initially, you may want to start collaborative working quite informally, with a few simple initiatives such as borrowing and lending resources. The important thing at this stage is to ensure that the organizations have a good 'fit' both operationally and culturally. If this works for all involved, then you might want to be more imaginative about the ways in which you could all cut costs or improve delivery and efficiency through your collaboration. And as long as your trustees can see clear advantages, there appear to be very few reasons why you shouldn't proceed.

According to the report, 'Strength in numbers – small charities' experience of working together', published by the Charity

Commission in 2010, collaborating with other charities works and brings real benefits. Of the 2,500 charities with incomes of less than £250,000 surveyed, nearly half (45 per cent) said they had collaborated with at least one other charity over the past two years; most commonly sharing information, joint fundraising and sharing equipment, and 82 per cent who had collaborated with others felt that it had been successful while 29 per cent thought it had been 'very' successful.

The benefits reported ranged from maintaining or improving services and enhancing reputation to identifying cost reductions and increased access to funding opportunities. Although many charities were motivated by a desire to improve services and reduce duplication, the main driver for collaboration, according to the report, was the presence of other charity partners in the local area with similar aims and objectives.

Too often in the past similar charities have viewed each other with suspicion whereas users found it difficult to differentiate. The Monty Python sketch about the 'The Peoples' Front of Judea' not speaking to the 'Judean Peoples' Front' springs to mind.

FINDING OTHER CHARITIES

Sometimes an opportunity to work with another charity just comes about naturally when your paths cross. If that's not the case but you have identified that collaboration would be a good route for your charity, then you can actively seek out other charities using the Find a Partner service at Funding Central (www.fundingcentral.org.uk), the sharing and mentoring service at the Small Charities Coalition (www.smallcharities. org.uk) or by using the Register of Charities held by the Charity Commission.

You are looking for a partner charity that will help you to further your charity's aims (as stated in your governing document), and whose input will help your beneficiaries. Before you get as far as agreeing to collaboration, you and your trustees need to satisfy yourselves that such an arrangement would be an appropriate use of your charity's money and energy.

If it looks to be a mutually beneficial working arrangement, then there are a few things to bear in mind before you proceed.

Firstly, you need to consider how compatible your work practices are and how you can complement each other – so which roles and responsibilities will each charity take on.

Once you have found a partner with whom you can work, you may want to formalize the arrangement and what you have both agreed to. It might just be a simple written agreement, often called a 'Memorandum of Understanding' or MoU; for example, if you agree to share use of an outdoor play area, or perhaps you group together to negotiate a good deal on a training programme or to get it tailored to the specific needs of the group. If the arrangement is more complex, for example collaborating to deliver training or services, then a fuller agreement or contract might be required.

FORMAL WAYS TO WORK TOGETHER

There are a variety of formal ways in which you can work with other charities to provide the best possible services for your and their beneficiaries.

The three most common structures are:

▶ The group structure

This is an association of separate organizations which allows charities to fulfil common purposes over a wide area, or deliver a complex range of services to beneficiaries. It is a formal arrangement whereby group members act as a collective but they keep their own individual name and identity, albeit that the group produces consolidated accounts. Such an arrangement can result in the provision of a wider and better range of services, financial savings and increased purchasing power, not to mention financial savings.

▶ The affiliated or federal structure

This is where a national charity exercises a degree of control over local charities which are its affiliates (members). Each local charity manages itself and has trustees who are responsible for its general control, while the national body has an advisory and supportive role. An example of an affiliated structure is the YMCA organization.

▶ The coalition structure

This is where a number of separate charities agree to work together for a common purpose, sometimes described as 'a partnership of equals'. The agreement may be only a temporary collaboration with a certain aim in mind, or it could be established on a more formal basis with a new association being set up.

SUCCESSFUL COLLABORATIONS

Once all parties involved in the collaboration have satisfied themselves that their independence will not be compromised and that it will further your charity's objects, then making sure all involved, including staff and stakeholders, are informed of what's going on and why you are collaborating can make the whole process run more smoothly.

Draw up an agreement that clarifies objectives, processes, roles and responsibilities to keep things clear and transparent. However, as long as both parties are clear that the collaboration is in the best interests of their charity's beneficiaries, then you are on the right track for a successful collaboration.

In bidding for income, one charity may become the lead organization fulfilling all the administration and reporting needs, while others focus on the operational delivery. In contracting situations, this leads to sub-contracts.

Remember this: Fundraising

You can fundraise on behalf of another charity, for instance, if it is for a major disaster appeal run by another charity, as long as your aims are consistent and you tell both the donors and the charity what you are raising funds for.

Try it now

Collaboration does not have to be limited to other charities. You could look at being involved with a commercial company if it is mutually beneficial. For example, you could collaborate with a house-builder who offers buyers a gardening service that is delivered by a charity that provides work experience for ex-offenders. The builder gets a selling advantage and the charity gets an outlet and avoids prejudice.

Linking with another charity

Linking two or more charities together is not the same as merging them. You can link charities where the charities involved have the same trustees or the charities are connected because they provide different aspects of the same service, for example, residents' welfare funds administered by the same residential care home.

Once your charities are linked, you have the advantage of only having to prepare one set of accounts and trustees' annual report and one annual return, because the linked charities share one charity number. One charity will become the 'reporting charity' which prepares the set of accounts for all the linked charities and it is the 'reporting charity' that retains its charity number (the other linked charities have the number plus a suffix). This loss of charity number can cause confusion, certainly initially, but such teething problems are soon overcome. The real limitation of linking charities is that because each linked charity keeps its own separate governing documents, you cannot combine assets or spend money on each other's aims. If this is not a drawback for you, then this can be a good compromise between a collaboration contract and an outright merger.

Merging with another charity

With all charities facing falling donations, funding and investment income, some are looking at mergers as a way to survive the recession. This can be a particularly attractive proposition for smaller charities with incomes of less than £500,000, which actually represent 95 per cent of all charities registered in England and Wales.

Since 2006, many of the legal obstacles to mergers were removed with the introduction of the Charities Act 2006, and since February 2009 a £16.5m fund has been made available by the Government to facilitate the process for voluntary organizations that wish to merge and modernize. For charities with a turnover of £750,000 or more, interest-free loans of up to £500,000 are available for assistance with mergers and merger advice.

The most high profile charity merger in recent times has been that of Help the Aged and Age Concern England to form Age

UK at the end of March 2009. Both charities were of a similar size and had similar goals – a prerequisite of merger – but they were funded and structured in different ways. Until that point, they had each filled the gap left by the other, but it became clear that further growth would only be possible if they went into direct competition with each other. A merger removed the need for such competition. In addition, it combined their complementary resources, enabled removal of duplication and produced a single organization that was better able to champion the growing needs of the older generation.

Both charities had shops, sold products and fundraised to varying degrees. The merger created three similar-sized income streams for Age UK, with the shops, fundraising and trading each generating about £50m of income. Most importantly, Age UK could now take the best from each organization to maximize its impact, for example, combining the fundraising database of HTA with the commercial expertise of ACE.

The Age UK merger was considered a big success with minimal redundancies and the minimum of brand confusion. If you are looking to merge with another charity, there are certain considerations you must take into account first.

CULTURE CLASHES

If you fear that there may be a culture clash between the two organizations, this needs to be addressed and resolved before you merge. It can be a good idea to draw up a formal list of merger objectives that everyone works towards.

Sometimes, it is the little things that can catch you out. Perhaps vocabulary used in one organization has a completely different meaning for staff in the other charity. Both organizations have to invest time in learning how the other operates. And it can also be a worthwhile exercise to revisit your own culture – are things done a certain way simply because they have always been done that way? Do you want it to work that way in the new culture?

COMPETING ROLES

Although you would be mistaken in thinking that the major reason for merger is to save money, in fact, the Charity

Commission estimates that only 37 per cent of charities merge for that reason – the majority – about 58 per cent – do so to improve service delivery. Nonetheless, when two charities merge, there is bound to be some duplication of roles, which means that staff will be competing for a limited number of positions in the new charity.

It can be hard to get people to co-operate and work together when potentially they could be in competition with each other for the same position. If the aim of the merger is growth, then hopefully redundancies can be kept to a minimum but not be entirely avoidable. It helps if you have an open and honest culture as this encourages staff to trust that the process will be fair and transparent. You can also make sure that everyone has a chance to make the case for their work or their way of doing things during the selection process.

It is best if all senior posts – chief executives, finance directors and indeed chair – go in to merger with no prescribed view of the outcome for them personally. One organization will not need two sets of leaders; it is as simple as that. You have to get on with it for the sake of the merged charity and remain aware that your role may not survive. C'est la vie.

BRANDING

Coming up with a name and a brand that is acceptable to all parties is one of the major stumbling blocks of any merger. Each charity will have its reputation, its brand image and there could be issues around copyright.

Not only must each charity be happy with the new name, but also the stakeholders, supporters and general public must accept the new image too, and understand the motives behind the merger. It's important that you get across to all concerned that the new charity can do more than the two charities could alone and that it will be better for the beneficiaries.

▶ **Tips for successful mergers**

1 The merger must be in the best interests of the charities' beneficiaries.

2 The charities involved must be compatible in objects, culture and values.

3 Effective communication with all stakeholders from the outset is vital – processes and outcomes should be clear to all involved.

4 The charities' trustees should be united in believing that the merger is the best way forward.

5 Identify the key roles and responsibilities in the merger process (both during transition and the end goal).

6 Communicate and negotiate in a way that reflects the interests of all parties.

7 Contact the Charity Commission at an early stage if advice is needed.

These tips are taken from the Charity Commission's Making Mergers Work document. To download the full document, go to the Charity Commission website.

REGISTER OF MERGED CHARITIES

The decision to merge should not be taken lightly. In the case of Age UK, it took six attempts over a period of ten years before the two organizations became one. But once everyone is agreed, and if all the legal requirements are met, namely that your governing document allows the merger and both charities have similar aims – then you can proceed.

If either of the charities involved in the merger receives significant legacy income, then you should consider registering the merger with the Charity Commission so that legacies and gifts can be transferred to the new charity. The problem arises when a will says the money must go to someone else if the original charity ceases to exist, so it can be wise to get legal advice before deciding to register the merger.

If you have no significant income from legacies and it's not on the cards in the future, then you only need to register the merger if a vesting declaration has been made. You can provide the necessary information to add your name to the merger list online.

Remember this: Transferring legacies

If both charities involved in the merger receive income in the form of
legacies, this must be transferred legally to the newly merged organization.

Try it now

Adding your names to the register of merged charities held by the
Charity Commission is voluntary but if the merger involves a 'vesting
declaration', which transfers property or other assets from one charity
to the other, then it is compulsory that you apply to be added to the
register of mergers.

Remember this: Pension debt and designated funds

If you are ever at the stage of considering a merger with another charity,
make sure that pensions are on your list from the start – pension debt
can make a big difference to the viability of any organization.

At some point, a charity may have received income for a specific purpose.
This may be held or invested in a designated fund. Ensure both parties are
aware of the binding nature, or not, of any designated funds.

Try it now

Not only will you need to consider legal transfer of any delivery contracts, but
also staff contracts. These will need to be aligned to a new single organization.

Closing your charity

There are a variety of reasons why charities wind up – and
they are not all bad. Clearly, some charities run into financial
difficulties and are forced to close. But many more are looking
at the decision to close because they have achieved the purpose
they were originally set up for, or perhaps they wish to become
a social enterprise company.

Even if you are facing a financial crisis, closure is not necessarily the only option available to you. Often, with specialist advice, insolvency or the need to wind up can be averted.

In 2011, the Charity Finance Directors' Group (CFDG) partnered with the NCVO to make its insolvency helpline publicly available to all charities. The helpline, which is run by PwC and MacIntyre Hudson and has been available to CFDG members for some time, helps organizations in crisis to prevent or mitigate the risk of insolvency. It also helps organizations that might be at the point of wind-up to understand the next steps.

However, for some, the decision to wind up is a positive one – anyone involved in the charity sector will have heard the expression, 'a successful charity is one that does itself out of business'. Sometimes, when a charity has achieved its mission, there is no longer a need to continue with the work. For others, they realize that there are other organizations and better ways to deliver their mission – keeping the charity going is not the only way to keep delivering the work.

If you are closing your charity under these circumstances – as a result of a proactive, measured and positive decision – then it is important to consider what positive legacy you can create after you have gone.

An excellent example of post-closure legacy is the Merseyside Basin Campaign (www.merseybasin.org.uk), which successfully cleared up the Mersey river network through collaborative action. Once their work was done, they set up a website containing an archive of photos, case studies, video clips and research papers, all of which are there to share the invaluable experience gained from 25 years of pioneering partnership working across multiple administrations.

Whether it is a decision forced by difficulties or taken willingly, closing an organization that has meant so much to you is always going to be emotional. The NCVO has a brilliant resource that shares the experiences of others who have been through the process and offers advice not only on the technicalities of closure but on how to deal with the unexpected emotions that closure can throw up.

Nonetheless, there is a great deal of work involved for the trustees and staff in order to fulfil the legal obligations of closing a charity, and you will naturally wish to minimize the impact on your beneficiaries.

Before seeking specialist legal advice on closure, check your charity's governing document. It may have a 'dissolution clause' which gives special instructions for what you need to do to close your charity. There is also detailed advice on the Charity Commission website.

Remember this: Deregistration

If your charity's annual income drops to less than £5,000 you can request to be removed from the Register of Charities, but you must be up-to-date with the filing responsibilities before your name can be removed. Thereafter, you can still call yourself a charity but not a 'registered' charity.

Try it now

Before you make a final decision regarding closing your charity, have you looked at other charities in your sector with similar objects who might make good candidates for a merger? In that way, you can still meet your users' needs and continue your work, albeit in a different guise.

Remember this: Notification

If you are a registered charity, you must let the Charity Commission know that you are going to close so that they can remove you from the Register of Charities.

Case study: Andrew Purvis, Chief Operating Officer at Virgin Unite, ex-CEO of Fairbridge

I argue that too many charities forget what their mission is – they are there to solve a problem that other parts of society are not addressing satisfactorily and ideally, when complete, they can close down. Sadly this rarely happens, however sustaining our MISSION rather than the ORGANIZATION was very much the guiding principle at Fairbridge in 2010 and early 2011. With Government making it clear that they were going to reduce significantly local authority spending from April 2011 and given that that represented 40 per cent of our overall funding, we knew we were in game changing times.

I was CEO at Fairbridge and as a management team we sat down and agreed that our responsibility was to ensure that the vital work we did helping young people transform their lives around the UK was the work that had to be protected. With dramatic changes to the then current funding available, we had to consider which scenarios and decisions would give our work the best possible chance to prosper.

We explored many different options but the most uncomfortable scenario slowly became the preferred option. This option - simply 'Merger' on the flip chart – entailed finding a merger partner who would benefit from having our programme interwoven into their work and who we felt would confidently weather the impending economic downturn better than we would be able to on our own. We wrestled with the decision – should we go alone and take the ship through the storm and hang the consequences. I certainly wrestled personally with the enormity of the decision, particularly as a relative newcomer – 2.5 years into my tenure and knowing the quality of the Fairbridge staff and the transformative power of our work. Ultimately it is about the beneficiaries of the work rather than the organization and I firmly believed that a merger executed effectively was our best chance of continuing and growing our work.

Another factor was speed – we were having the internal conversation while we were financially strong. In mid-2010 our fundraising team was doing a good job and reserves were at a reasonable level. It was clearly better to have discussions with a potential partner while we were in good financial shape rather than to wait and potentially be in a less good place.

The Trustees and management team discussed the concept and agreed that the thinking made sense and this would become the strategic priority. We listed, researched and marked various contending charities as the ideal partner and for a number of reasons the Prince's Trust came out on top.

We had the necessary conversations and fortunately the Prince's Trust's Chairman and Chief Executive quickly saw the logic of the merger in very much the same way that we did. They enjoyed a higher percentage of private sector funding and therefore had to be convinced that they were not 'catching a falling knife' as local authority funding pots dried up. The fact that our programmes did link together neatly and Fairbridge's positive overall financial outlook helped convince everyone that the merger was in the best interest of both organizations.

Once agreed in principle there was a six month period firstly of due diligence and then merger planning in two 3 month instalments. Both were done professionally and rigorously and the merger was consummated some six months after the first meeting to propose the idea.

I then stepped aside as had been agreed in that very first meeting. It felt weird – a mixture of relief and huge sadness. Sadness to walk away from an organization that was so special, sadness that I was not there to do my bit to make the merger a success, and sadness because I knew there would be changes and that some of them would inevitably be uncomfortable. Against that, the relief of hopefully giving the organization the very best chance of growing and developing as part of the enlarged Prince's Trust.

On reflection what would I share?

1 Do act in the best interests of the charity's mission – it is not about simply sustaining the organization and meeting payroll.
2 Be bold in your strategic decision making. Too many third sector organizations are inherently conservative in my experience.
3 Move quickly and move while you are strong if you are to make a radical shift in your strategy.
4 Think carefully about how you bring the organization with you. They will see the context very differently to you – be prepared to listen and be receptive but also defend your case.
5 Mergers are a bit like turkeys voting for Christmas. There will be attrition at the top. Think how you prepare for/sweeten this reality.
6 Scenario plan as fully as you can – this will prepare you for the many unforeseen outcomes.
7 Be very clear at the outset of any negotiation on the non-negotiables. And the list is probably much shorter than you initially think it will be.

Focus points

Collaboration with another charity can help to pool resources, improve services and cut costs, so you can operate more economically.

Collaboration can be informal or formal.

Linking with another charity is an option for those charities sharing trustees and that are already connected.

Merging charities can benefit end-users, save on costs and remove duplication of services.

Closing a charity is not always as a result of difficulties. It can be a positive move.

Next step

Having looked at ways to streamline and make your organization more efficient, perhaps by collaboration or merger, we are now looking at measures you can take if you want to diversify your charity's remit by widening its objectives.

13

Making changes

In this chapter you will learn:

- ▶ *When it is a good idea to change your charity's name*
- ▶ *What to do if you want to change or widen your charity objectives*
- ▶ *How to update your scheme of arrangements*
- ▶ *What to do if you want to amend your governing documents*
- ▶ *How to become a charitable company or charitable incorporated organization (CIO).*

You may feel that you need to make some fairly radical changes to your charity and how it is run to adapt to the new economic climate, but it requires a great deal of research, forethought and, in many cases, permission from the regulator – the Charity Commission – before you can proceed.

In this chapter, we are going to look at some of the major changes to the organization and running of your charity that you might wish or need to consider at some point.

Changing your charity name

There are a variety of reasons why a charity might decide to change its name but the most common motive is an organizational rebrand. As we saw in Chapter 7, a charity's brand is of utmost importance in convincing potential supporters of its worth, so rebranding is a risky exercise and quite often expensive. When it works well, it can pay dividends, but most charities see an initial dip in income and awareness in the year following the rebranding.

If you want to rebrand, your first port of call is to check your charity's governing document – if it includes a procedure for changing the name, you will need to follow it exactly.

Over and above that, you would want of course to do substantial research before selecting a new name, probably with the help of a professional marketing agency. They will carry out an online search for existing names – both on the charity register and as trademarks – but be aware that such searches will only bring up exact matches and not necessarily names that are similar.

At the opposite end of the spectrum, if the name is too generic, it will not be possible to register it as a trademark too. Checking you can trademark your name and register it with the Charity Commission is the first step before you spend large amounts of money on creating a new brand, marketing strategies and registering website domain names.

Changing your name is likely to attract criticism and upset some existing supporters, so it is only worth considering if it is part of a wider change in your charity's remit and the way you do things – changing your charity name for the sake of it is not a worthwhile exercise. A name change is a way of trying to shift or consolidate perceptions about your brand but it is a hard thing to get right.

Once your trustees, stakeholders and supporters are happy with the new name and they understand the motives behind the rebrand, then you can start the marketing campaign to get it accepted by a wider public audience.

Before the campaign can start, you must notify the Charity Commission that you want to change your charity's name, citing the date of the meeting at which the trustees and/or members accepted the name change and, if your charity is a company, the date of the certificate of incorporation showing the new name, and they will then update the Register of Charities. You can do this via an online form on the regulator's website. You would also be well advised to consult staff as you do not want to disenfranchise your greatest asset – staff goodwill.

Try it now

You may well have registered a domain name for your charity, but make sure there is not a similar name in use. If you are randomname.org.uk and there is a randomname.org or even randomname.co.uk or .com, quite a lot of potential traffic could get diverted. Buy as many suffixes as you feel necessary to protect your web name.

Try it now

If you get a design agency to design a logo for your new name, make sure you have the rights over that logo. If ownership of the intellectual property remains with the designer, you could end up paying through the nose to use it for different purposes, such as on your website.

Remember this: Fallen figurehead

One of the worst fates that could befall a charity that does great things for its beneficiaries is if its figurehead – its founder, its namesake – is disgraced. This has been in the public eye in recent months due to the scandals surrounding Jimmy Savile and Lance Armstrong, both of whom had charities in their name. In these circumstances, a change of name is almost certainly the best course of action because the charity will be forever tainted if not. Sadly, the two charities in Savile's name decided a name change was not enough and took the more extreme route of announcing their closure. Meanwhile, the Lance Armstrong Foundation, Livestrong, thought they could weather the scandal because of their global reputation, but in May 2013, Nike cut its ties with the charity, ending a nine-year-long relationship – clearly the future will not be easy for them. Of course, such cases are extremely rare, but Savile and Armstrong are timely reminders that celebrity reputations tumble at lightning speed and having a risk management plan in place for such eventualities can be a shrewd move.

Changing what your charity does

When you first formed your charity, you drew up documents outlining its purposes – its object – and the ways in which you wanted to operate, and these declarations became your governing document.

Over the fullness of time, however, the needs of your charity or its beneficiaries may change and unforeseen eventualities may arise. In this case, you may wish to modify what you do and the governing document may need to change accordingly. How you go about this depends on the size and nature of your charity, as the rules differ depending on whether you are a small or large unincorporated charity, or a charitable company. The key principle is that you must always consult your stakeholders.

UPDATING GOVERNING DOCUMENTS

The governing document should reflect how your charity actually operates today. Sometimes the purposes and administrative procedures outlined in your governing document become out of date and, in this case, the trustees need to amend them to reflect the true situation.

If you always bear in mind that an individual or group is investing in your charity believing in what you say you are doing, then you will understand this needs to be accurately represented.

There may of course be conditions to be met in order to change the governing document. If there is a power of amendment in the original governing document, this makes things much easier because you simply proceed according to its instructions. If you cannot make the change under a power in the governing document, then you may be able to do so under the powers that are available in charity law.

As a general rule of thumb, if you are an unincorporated charity with an income of less than £10,000 (and you don't have designated land), you can change both the administrative provisions and the purposes yourselves. If you are an unincorporated charity with an income of more than £10,000, you can change the administrative provision but changes to the purposes will either require a suitable power in the existing governing document or a scheme from the Charity Commission (see below).

If you decide to change your governing document and your charity is registered with the Charity Commission, then you will need to notify it of the change and provide an updated copy of the document.

Remember this: Charity powers

Although, in broad terms, trustees can make changes to the powers and procedures of their charity's governing document relating to the admin of the charity – things like changing the charity's name, borrowing and investing money, co-operating with other charities, membership, etc. – there are safeguards in place such as passing a resolution or being required to notify the Charity Commission, so it is worth seeking advice. If the charity has members, the trustees may need the permission of the members to make the changes.

CHANGING YOUR PURPOSES

Your charity's purposes (sometimes called aims) tell the world about the character of your charity and a change to your purposes should not be undertaken lightly. There are situations where it is fitting – perhaps circumstances or society has changed. A charity set up after the influenza epidemic after the First World War, for example, would have re-examined its purposes when the number of people needing help dropped. It might have decided to extend its work to cover the families of those who died during the epidemic, or to help influenza sufferers in another country.

It may be that, through your work in a specific area, you find that another user group will benefit from your services. It makes sense to include them while not diluting your purpose or brand.

Radical change to purposes is not encouraged. Rather you should be looking for something that is similar in character to the old set of purposes and that will serve your charity's best interests. And, as in the beginning, they must be exclusively charitable in their wording.

For unincorporated charities with an income of less than £10,000 (and without designated land), trustees can amend the purposes by passing a resolution with at least two-thirds of those who vote. You then inform the Charity Commission using their online form, explaining what you will do to achieve the new purposes and when the change was agreed. As long as there is no objection or request for further information from the Commission or any of your key stakeholders, then the resolution takes effect 60 days after the Commission receives it.

For unincorporated charities with incomes of more than £10,000, you can only change your charity's purposes if your governing document allows it, in which case you follow the requirements that it sets out. As before, the amended object will have to be exclusively charitable and you will need to inform the Charity Commission of the change. If there is no provision in the governing documents, you will need to apply to the Charity Commission for a scheme to make the changes.

GETTING A SCHEME

A scheme is a legal document, made by the Charity Commission, to add to, replace or amend provisions set out in a charity's governing document – and it's a last resort. The other routes to amending your governing documents mentioned above are much simpler, if they are available to you.

If that is not the case, then your trustees must apply to the Commission for a scheme or they could apply to the High Court, but this is generally an expensive option. Be prepared to explain why you need to carry out the changes and what your new objects might cover with your contact at the Commission and they will advise and agree a broad outline of the best approach. You can then formally apply for a scheme and the Charity Commission will then decide upon the terms of the scheme in consultation with your trustees and any other key personnel.

Once the scheme is authorized and comes into effect, a copy of the signed papers should be given to every trustee and there may be a stipulation that the scheme should be displayed publicly for a set period, but this is only likely if there have been significant objections before the scheme was authorized.

Depending on how complicated the scheme is, it usually takes a number of weeks between applying for and receiving your authorized scheme, and the regulator does not charge for this service. The only real costs to you, apart from staff time, are if you pay for professional advice in connection with the scheme or if you have to publish notices, and in making copies for the trustees.

Remember this: Scheme

A scheme and the changes in it to amend a charity's governing document will only be made by the Charity Commission when there is absolutely no other route available to the trustees and if the changes cannot be made any other way.

Becoming a charitable company or charitable incorporated organization (CIO)

As your income grows, you may want to change the structure of your charity, and it may well be that you decide to convert to become a charitable company or to the new structure that's now available, namely a charitable incorporated organization (CIO).

In both instances, the new structure will offer trustees much greater protection in terms of personal liability for its debts or legal action. It is hoped that becoming a charitable company or CIO will make it easier to recruit new trustees, which has in the past proved difficult for unincorporated charities where the trustees have faced personal risks. Modern contracting arrangements also require all parties to outline who is responsible for any liabilities. This should be an organization, or structure, and not individuals. Changing to a new structure can also represent a good opportunity to revamp your constitution.

Moreover, as a charitable company or CIO, your charity can employ staff, own land or enter into contracts in its own name, as the law considers a company to have the same legal status as a person. The advantage of a CIO as compared to a charitable company is that they have the same limited liability as a company, but a CIO only reports to the Charity Commission, filing one set of accounts and one annual report, and does not have to file to Companies House (for which there is a charge).

Obviously, after conversion, it will entail filing some more paperwork, but many medium-sized charities in particular could benefit substantially from making the conversion (probably less so for very small charities who are not concerned with liabilities such as contracts, property, investments and employees).

CONVERTING INTO A CHARITABLE COMPANY
The process is quite straightforward. Firstly, you must set up and register a new company with Companies House and then you register your new company as a charity with the Charity Commission. Finally, and only after you make sure that your original charity has no outstanding debts or liabilities that need paying, you can close your original unincorporated charity, unless you decide to keep it as a linked charity or register a merger.

CONVERTING TO A CIO
There is no conversion process as such at the present time. You have to set up a new CIO, and then transfer all of the

assets and liabilities of the existing charity across. Since the new CIO will have charitable objects that are identical to those of the existing unincorporated charity and the name is remaining the same, this process shouldn't be too arduous or time-consuming.

As when forming any new CIO, you can create a constitution either in the 'Foundation' format, where the trustees are the same as the members, or the 'Association' format, where the trustees and members may be different and where there may be a much larger body of members. The Charity Commission provides model constitutions for CIOs, which you can use and amend as necessary to make suitable for conversion from an existing charity.

Once the new CIO has been formed, the trustees of the existing charity will need to obtain the approval of the members of the charity to dissolve the charity and transfer its assets to the new CIO.

Changing from an unincorporated charity to a CIO also affects the staff and their contracts will have to be transferred across. If you had a defined benefit pension scheme before, then you should seek specialist advice before the transfer takes place, as this may be a notifiable event, in which case you must notify the pensions regulator and, most importantly, your pension provider in writing.

Staff should be consulted in advance before the transfer and given written notice of the changes. Technically, it is a change of employer and therefore the provisions of Transfer of Undertakings (Protection of Employment) Regulations (TUPE) will apply, so I would recommend that you get employment advice. In practical terms, the change of structure should not affect the everyday working lives of the staff at all.

Finally, the trustees of the new CIO must notify everybody dealing with the charity of the change that has taken place. If they fail to do so, the charity will not be able to take full advantage of the benefits of limited liability which incorporation brings with it.

Remember this: Charitable company

You cannot currently convert from a charitable company into a CIO but this is in the pipeline. Once the Charity Commission provides this option, it could well be worth considering as they will have less administration going forward and will be dealing with just one regulator.

Try it now

When you transfer assets over to the new charity, you become a new legal entity and will be issued with a different charity number and so you will have to notify your bank, creditors, HMRC and any relevant government departments of the change.

Case study: Nick Marr, Group Chief Executive of Henshaws: Changing the legal status

There are many reasons to change the legal status of your charity, but at Henshaws, the main reasons were to limit the liability of the trustees in order to be able to recruit new trustees and to allow us to enter into modern contracting arrangements.

Modern contracts and partnerships require the liabilities to be clear and it was becoming apparent that having individual trustees who were personally liable for larger contracts was not going to be considered reasonable for our potential partners.

We had seven trustees yet we really need about eleven to ensure that all of the key areas of governance are covered and the existing trustees don't end up doing everything. Trustees need to be protected from unnecessary liability and these days prospective trustees are very aware of this. Therefore the charity needed to consider incorporation of some sort.

There was a major problem caused by the terms of our pension agreement as any changes in the legal status – no matter how positive – would technically have required us to meet the pension deficit calculated at that time. This amounted to millions of pounds, and presented a 'cleft stick' for the trustees.

To get around the problem, we firstly opened negotiation with the pensions' provider and then sought expert charity legal advice. The timing of our talks with the pensions' provider was key as they were looking for a long-term solution to their member organizations facing increasing deficits and also wanted to provide a credible vehicle for pension auto-enrolment being rolled out by the Government. After a long period of negotiation and specialist legal pension advice, it was agreed that we could change the legal status, change our pension provision and not trigger the debt.

Expert charity legal advice is hard to find, whereas legal advice is not. For many years, the charity has used the same lawyers and, in most areas, they are excellent. In the case of charity incorporation, they are not experts. So we found lawyers who were, we agreed a set fee and set about the task in hand. In the event, the most appropriate model for Henshaws was for the trustee body to be incorporated rather than the whole organization. A crucial element throughout this process was that our lawyers had a good and effective relationship with the Charity Commission and together they worked out the most appropriate model to follow. I've always found the Commission extremely helpful in terms of regulation and it has always been happy to help in terms of compliance with regulation, but cannot necessarily tell you how to implement the process. The analogy I'd make is that of a traffic warden who can tell you whether you can or cannot park in a particular place, but will not necessarily advise on how to get your car in to the space. That said, I've found that, if you outline what you believe to be your options, the Commission will advise on what has appeared most successful in the past.

During this process, we also felt it was prudent to take the opportunity to modernize and broaden the charity's object. This required consultation of all the major stakeholders: staff, supporters and most importantly the members. In our case, the members were those individuals who have financially contributed to the charity. We sent out publications to our members outlining the changes and the reasoning behind it and sought their feedback. We also invited members to our Annual General Meeting and had a separate consultation meeting to allow anyone to voice their views. All of this was done with regular advice from the Charity Commission and ensuring that everyone had the opportunity to participate. In the end, we received two communications about what we proposed to do, neither was an objection but both commented about additional work we could consider. Both of these pieces of correspondence were discussed, responses sent and copies of all correspondence sent to the Commission.

At the outset of the process, we set up a working group consisting of the chief executive, finance director and three trustees: the chairman, vice chair and treasurer, to navigate this path and discuss the areas in detail. This worked very successfully and ensured that neither trustee meetings nor senior management meetings became unnecessarily clogged with technical detail.

In the end the trustee body was incorporated and the pension provider was kept happy. We updated our object, our membership and governing practices. It took four years, the hard work of many staff and trustees, but we've just recruited our first batch of new trustees.

Focus points

A change to the name of your charity is usually as a result of a rebranding exercise, and should be thoroughly market researched first.

It is possible to update your governing documents if they become out-dated or unrepresentative , for example.

Usually it is possible for the trustees to change your charity's purposes, as set out in the governing document.

If this is not allowed for in the governing document, you can still change your purposes but you would have to apply to the Charity Commission for a scheme.

You can change from being an unincorporated charity or trust to become a charitable company or CIO, and the process is known as incorporation.

Next step

That just about winds up all the information that I think you need to successfully run your charity. It only leaves me to review what the future holds for the charity sector in the next chapter before we part company.

14

The future is bright

In this chapter you will learn that:

▶ *There is tentative optimism in the sector*
▶ *Charities are adapting in response to change*
▶ *Many see that the future lies in getting younger people involved*
▶ *Charities are much more in the public consciousness now*

By this stage of the book, you should hopefully have a good idea of what is involved in setting up and running a charity, and not just the need for detailed planning, but also the need for planning strategically in order to achieve your aim. You will also hopefully have a grasp of what is required to keep your charity moving forward and how you can best help your beneficiaries or your specific cause.

Undoubtedly, there will be times when you find it tough and you will wonder why you ever started. I hope those occasions will be few. It has been a tough few years for the charity sector and we are not through 'the perfect storm' of increasing need and limited resources yet. Charities are faced with uncertainty over funding, increasing costs and the need to attract more donations. And with government cuts hitting hard, it is going to be economically difficult for a few more years to come.

However, as someone who has been involved in the charity sector for nigh on 30 years, I can see that there is also good news to share. The increase in corporate confidence is beginning to be echoed in the charity sector. There is tentative optimism in the air. In fact, a new report, 'Managing in the "New Normal" – Adapting to Uncertainty' – published in March 2013 shows that charities are growing less pessimistic about the future despite the tough fundraising environment and a rising demand for services. This report, the sixth in the *Managing in a Downturn* series, produced annually by the Charity Finance Group, the Institute of Fundraising and PwC shows that 46 per cent of respondents reported an energized or optimistic team and 61 per cent said they were optimistic for the future of their charities.

And a clue to this new-found confidence is in the title of the report – 'Adapting to Uncertainty'. Somehow, charities have adapted to the challenges, have responded to the changes and have innovated in the best interests of their beneficiaries. They have sought new ways to increase income, either from fundraising or trading, and while not losing sight of the charity's mission, they have thought strategically and moved swiftly to continue to function and, in some cases, to achieve success in challenging times.

For some, the adaptation has taken the form of looking to develop partnerships and perhaps consider a merger with another charity as a way to improve their prospects. The opportunities for economies of scale and for greater impact presented by the merger option are proving irresistible to some smaller charities.

Other charities are looking to the future by trying to attract the next generation of donors. To do so, they are actively involving the young, engaging those in the 20 to 30 age bracket in particular. With increasing numbers of young people looking to get on the work ladder and build their experience and CV, the arrangement is mutually beneficial.

And in the broader context, it is a very positive time to be involved in the charity sector. There is heightened public awareness about what charities do, thanks in part to the increased popularity and availability of the internet, so that people are better informed and have easier access to ways to donate.

Cash-strapped charities are realizing that it is easier to weather the storm together rather than to face it in isolation and we are seeing a greater degree of co-operation within the sector than ever before.

The sector is also attracting a new generation of trustees and charity workers who have a more modern, entrepreneurial approach to charity. It is proving to be a much-needed shot in the arm for the sector at this challenging time.

Finally, the huge success of high profile campaigns such as Sport Relief and Children in Need and other charity fundfeeders such as Help for Heroes and Just Giving has helped to raise the profile of and provide easily-accessible mechanisms for public giving. This, in part, is perhaps responsible for the rise in public participation and involvement in fundraising activities such as Fun Runs – since Race for Life started in 1994, an incredible six million participants have raised over £493 million, more than any other UK event series raising money to fund cancer research. In addition, the growing emphasis on and growing understanding of corporate social responsibility means that you are more likely to be involved in supporting a chosen charity through your work than ever before.

A more discerning public can also play its part in changing the face of the charity sector. As the Director of Legal and Compliance at the Charity Commission, Kenneth Dibble says, 'If the sector as a whole is to reach the best standard of governance, we need a culture change. We should approach charity giving in the way we approach buying a new household appliance – as careful, responsible consumers... Charities and think-tanks such as New Philanthropy Capital have done great work in urging big ticket donors to ask big questions before supporting a charity, but that approach should spread to charity donors, no matter how deep their pockets.'

Although trustee boards and chief executives still have a tough task ahead and need to consider the range of options open to them, it is good to see that the third sector is showing signs of optimism and new growth. The one thing that has stayed constant through all this evolution is the fact that the reward for being involved in a charity and seeing the effects of your endeavours is as great as ever. There is nothing to beat it.

And so the last word should go to the reason why I am still working for a charity after all these years. Let's hear from one of the beneficiaries of Henshaws as we come to the end of the book – but before we do, all that is left for me to say is Good Luck to you in all your charitable ventures.

Case study: Andrew Laidler, service user of Henshaws Society for Blind People

There is no doubt that Henshaws has been fundamental in giving me back my life. My eyes have been subject to a multitude of complications from birth, including congenital cataracts and glaucoma, and by the time I was 4 years old I was registered blind. I remember being confused and asking my dad what was wrong with my eyes, to which he replied, 'Just about everything.'

In December 2007 I suffered from a detached retina which I had surgery for. I cannot begin to describe how torturous this time was for me. I suffered from sleep deprivation and the fear of going blind led to severe and acute depression that came on very suddenly. During this time

I started to have hallucinations and became suicidal. Finally, my retina became detached again and everything went dark. I'd never felt so alone.

A member of Henshaws staff from their team in Newcastle was referred to me. She came to my house but I have to admit I was pretty rude at first. She was very patient though and persevered with me to get the help I needed. I was admitted to hospital for three months as I had become a danger to myself. Henshaws staff trained the nurses to understand my unique case and after starting to feel a bit better I decided to give Henshaws and their Skillstep course a try.

It was a complete breakthrough for me. I never thought I'd use a computer again but very quickly I was surfing the internet, using specialist screen reading software. What I enjoyed most about Henshaws was their dedication to treating me as an individual and I rebuilt my self-worth and self-belief, after it had been completely destroyed.

My journey with Henshaws changed my life and Skillstep gave me a new-found enthusiasm for living. I thought my world was over at one point but being blind won't ever hold me back again. Of course I still have days when I miss seeing my wife's face but it hasn't stopped me from getting stuck into life again.

With my confidence rebuilt and new skills learnt I decided to set up my own business. I don't believe anything is impossible any more. My ambition is to become a millionaire so that I can be a source of inspiration to others. It might not happen, but that doesn't matter. After all, it's the journey that counts.

Andrew Laidler, Henshaws Service User, www.henshaws.org.uk

Useful contacts
and addresses

Association of Chief Executives of Voluntary Organizations (ACEVO)

London Office:
Regent's Wharf
8 All Saints Street
London, N1 9RL
Tel: 020 7014 4600
Leeds Office:
Foundation Tennant Hall
Blenheim Grove
Leeds
LS2 9ET
Tel: 0113 243 2333

ACF (Association of Charitable Foundations)

Central House
14 Upper Woburn Place
London WC1H 0AE
Tel: 020 7255 4499
www.acf.org.uk

Charities Aid Foundation (CAF)

25 Kings Hill Avenue
Kings Hill
West Malling
Kent
ME19 4TA
Tel: 0300 123 000
www.cafonline.org

Charities Evaluation Services

www.ces-vol.org.uk
Charity Commission for England and Wales
PO Box 1227
Liverpool
L69 3UG
www.charity-commission.gov.uk

Charity Commission for Northern Ireland (CCNI)

257 Lough Road,
Lurgan,
Craigavon BT66 6NQ
Tel: 0282 832 0220
www.charitycommissionni.org.uk

Charity Law Foundation

www.charitylawassociation.org.uk
email: admin@charitylawassociation.org.uk
Tel: 01634 373253

Charity Trustee Networks (CTN)

www.trusteenet.org.uk

Chartered Institute of Personnel and Development (CIPD)

www.cipd.co.uk

Community Interest Companies

www.cicregulator.gov.uk

Community Matters

www.communitymatters.org.uk

Directory of Social Change

24 Stephenson Way
London
NW1 2DP
Tel: 0845 077 7707
www.dsc.org.uk

Economic and Social Research Council (ESRC) – Advice and funding opportunities

www.esrc.ac.uk

European Social Fund (ESF)

www.esf.gov.uk

Financial Conduct Authority

www.fca.org.uk

Get Legal

www.getlegal.org.uk

Free online advice on legal structures and issues such as governance for charities, social enterprises and co-ops

HM Revenue and Customs

HMRC Charities
St John's House
Merton Road
Liverpool
L75 1BB
Tel: 0845 302 0203
www.hmrc.gov.uk

HMRC Charities Helpline – 0845 302 0203

Institute for Public Policy Research (IPPR)

4th Floor,
14 Buckingham Street,
London WC2N 6DF
www.ippr.org
Tel: 020 7470 6100

Law Works

www.lawworks.org.uk/

Provides free legal help to individuals and community groups who cannot afford to pay for it and who are unable to access legal aid.

National Association for Voluntary and Community Action (NAVCA)

The Tower
2 Furnival Square Sheffield
S1 4QL
Tel: 0114 278 6636
www.navca.org.uk

National Council for Voluntary Organizations (NCVO)

Society Building
8 All Saints Street
London N1 9RL
www.ncvo-vol.org.uk
Tel: 020 7713 6161
(merged with Volunteering England)

Office for Civil Society (OCS) (formerly the Office of the Third Sector)

www.civilsociety.co.uk

Office of the Scottish Charity Regulator (OSCR)

2nd Floor
Quadrant House
9 Riverside Drive
Dundee
DD1 4NY
www.oscr.org.uk

Small Charities Coalition

24 Stephenson Way,
London NW1
www.smallcharities.org.uk

Third Sector Research Centre

www.tsrc.ac.uk

Wales Council for Voluntary Action (WCVA)

Baltic House
Mount Stuart Square
Cardiff
CF10 5FH
Tel: 029 2043 1700
www.wcva.org.uk

Third Sector European Network

www.tsen.org.uk

▶ **Volunteering**

Do-It

www.do-it.org.uk

Rural Community Councils

www.acre.org.uk

Volunteering England

www.volunteering.org.uk

▶ **Fundraising**

Arts Council of England

www.artscouncil.org.uk

Arts Council of Northern Ireland

www.artscouncil-ni.org

Arts Council of Wales

www.artswales.org.uk

Big Lottery Fund

www.biglotteryfund.org.uk

Lottery grants specifically for charities, voluntary and community groups

British Film Institute

www.bfi.org.uk

CAF Bank

www.cafonline.org

Charity Bank

www.charitybank.org

Charity Retail Association

www.charityshops.org.uk

Common Purpose – Leadership courses

www.commonpurpose.org

Co-operative and Community Finance

www.co-opfinance.co-op

Fit for Funding

www.fit4funding.org.uk

Heritage Lottery Fund

www.hlf.org.uk

Institute of Fundraising

Park Place, 12 Lawn Lane, London SW8 1UD
Tel: 020 7840 1000
www.institute-of-fundraising.org.uk

Locality

www.locality.org.uk

Lottery Funding

www.lotteryfunding.org.uk

Lottery Good Causes

www.lotterygoodcauses.org.uk
Tel: 0845 275 0000
For information on all lottery distributors

Online Gift Aid Filing

www.hmrc.gov.uk/charitiesonline

Scottish Arts Council

www.scottisharts.org.uk

Social Enterprise UK

www.socialenterprise.org.uk

Sport England

www.sportengland.org

Sport Scotland

www.sportscotland.org.uk

Sports Council for Northern Ireland

www.sportni.net

Sports Council for Wales

www.sportwales.org.uk

Unity Trust Bank

www.unity.co.uk

▶ **Corporate fundraising**

Arts and Business

www.artsandbusiness.bitc.org.uk

Bar Pro Bono (website for volunteering barristers and solicitors)

www.barprobono.org.uk

Business in the Community and Pro Help

www.bitc.org.uk

Company Giving

www.companygiving.org.uk

Professional4Free (professionals who give free help to voluntary and community groups)

www.professionals4free.org.uk

School for Social Enterprise

www.the-sse.org

Index